RENEWING THE REPUBLIC

First published in 2011 by
Liberties Press
Guinness Enterprise Centre | Taylor's Lane | Dublin 8
Tel: +353 (1) 415 1224
www.libertiespress.com | info@libertiespress.com

Trade enquiries to Gill & Macmillan Distribution
Hume Avenue | Park West | Dublin 12
T: +353 (1) 500 9534 | F: +353 (1) 500 9595 | E: sales@gillmacmillan.ie

Distributed in the UK by
Turnaround Publisher Services
Unit 3 | Olympia Trading Estate | Coburg Road | London N22 6TZ
T: +44 (0) 20 8829 3000 | E: orders@turnaround-uk.com

Distributed in the United States by
Dufour Editions | PO Box 7 | Chester Springs | Pennsylvania 19425

ISBN: 978-1-907593-21-5
2 4 6 8 10 9 7 5 3 1
A CIP record for this title is available from the British Library.

Cover design by Sin É Design
Internal design by Liberties Press
Printed by ScandBook

RENEWING THE REPUBLIC

MICHAEL D. HIGGINS

Contents

1.

Recovering the Promise of a Real Republic

'That which has failed must not be repaired.'

I wish to thank those who have sat in the Chair at different stages, for their courtesy and kindness to me over a very long period. I have been here in this Chamber for twenty-five years, with nine years in the Seanad, and since I first stood for election forty-two years ago. I am indebted not just for the courtesy of Members of this House, the staff and the ushers and others, but also, on occasion, for their kindness as well. *Gabhaim buíochas ó chroí leo agus chomh maith le mo chomhleacaithe thar na blianta.*

This evening I want to take advantage of the wide range of speeches that have preceded mine, including those on Dáil reform. Nevertheless, I wish to concentrate on what I believe makes up some of the contextual background to what we are discussing today. I wish the next government well. It is a government I hope to look at from a distance. I have already said I am very grateful for the kindness and courtesy of my colleagues in this House over the years, and I hope not to be saying a goodbye to them. If I succeed in getting the Labour Party nomination for the presidency, I look forward to meeting them all in their constituencies in a less formal setting.

When I first stood for election in 1969, I was very conscious of something that is important to me. I was leaving an academic world in which I had spent a great deal of time, and on which I had expended a great deal of anxiety in order to secure entry. People from backgrounds such as mine did not go to university, did not qualify in other universities, and certainly did not teach in universities. I left that world to participate in public life, which was part of the tradition of my family. I wish people from all walks of life took part in politics and in public life. It is very important to act in the public space with whatever, as Connolly would put it, are the gifts of hand or brain one has, and to deliver it for one's fellow citizens. I was conscious in 1969, however, of the great failure of a country that then called itself a republic. I believe no real republic has been created in Ireland. The failure has been of three kinds. There has been a failure in making political power republican; a failure in making republican any kind of administrative power; and a failure with regard to communicative power. Without being technical about each of these, I think that those who wanted Ireland to be independent would have envisaged a country in which there would be a far greater distribution of power, that it would not be confined solely to the exercise of parliamentary democracy.

Parliamentary democracy is incredibly important. For many years, people in Ireland struggled to have their own parliament and struggled to participate in it. But there is more to political power than voting once every four or five years; there is the exercise of power in every dimension of life. If a real republic had been founded, we should have been spending decades extending and deepening political power. To the credit of the Labour Party, that has been its intention and aspiration, however achieved, since it was founded in 1912. With regard to administrative power, it is quite appalling that there was no real change from the time the Treasury dominated in the olden days in the handover to the Department of Finance.

As a political scientist, I find it quite extraordinary that so much attention has focused on changing the electoral system and so little on the structure of Cabinet power. There is no constitutional basis for the hegemony of the Department of Finance; it was a practice that flowed seamlessly from the British Treasury and was adopted without question. If one wanted to effect radical change, one would break the connection between the monopoly enjoyed by the government of the day and Parliament. One would allow, for example, the establishment of a committee system with the right to initiate and change legislation. If one wanted to go further, as in the Scandinavian model, it would be to allow committees to have limited budgetary powers, thus ensuring that people who came into politics would have a career in politics separate from being on the front bench, if in Opposition, or being in Cabinet, if in government. These are real reforms, but they are empty and missing from the discourse. I have the impression that even though the Labour Party has produced 140 proposals which I strongly support, including in particular its proposals on citizenship, I find, generally, that there is an element of fright in what those elected are suggesting, as if they are offering themselves for reform, as if that was the major problem. That is not the problem.

I will give my opinion on where I think this is going, having spent my lifetime not just in elected politics but also in academic politics and the social sciences – another area of great failure. I say this as a founding member of the Irish Sociological Association and the Irish Political Science Association. One need only watch television and listen to radio to know what is happening internationally. A significant price is already being paid for the broken connection between the aspirations of the people of this planet and those who take decisions on their behalf. The distinguished political scientist Jürgen Habermas has suggested that people can be invited to be bound by rules and by decisions in which they have had a chance to consciously participate. In one part of the world after another, we have the assumption that rational parliaments will be able to solve global problems such as the food crisis, the environmental crisis, the energy crisis, or whatever.

At the same time, very serious people are suggesting that it is parliament that is irrational, and that markets are rational, when in fact all the evidence shows that it is the flow of international market capital which is completely unaccountable and is irrational. There is no evidence since the Crash in the 1920s in the United States, which can show one jot of evidence, as both Professor Samuels Senior and Junior have stated, that the markets are rational. There is strong evidence for the speculative consequences of markets.

On the other hand, people have put all their trust in parliaments, and all over the world parliament is losing. In the European Union, for instance, we are in the gravest danger of sinking back to a common market rather than a Europe beyond wars, which might have been a Europe of all the citizens. The 'citizen deficit' in Europe is its most serious failure. That is why those who want to defend their banks, be they French presidents or German chancellors, are defending their francs rather than the possibilities of Europe. They have put us in so much danger as regards the European project.

There was a great opportunity missed to build a real inclusive republic in Ireland, which would have reformed the relationship of Cabinet to the Dáil structures, that would have had a democratic, local government, that would have allowed opportunities for participation. There has been a political failure to establish a republic. There has also been an administrative failure, whereby administrative structures are hierarchical and patriarchal. I listen to those speaking about the clash between being a legislator and being a representative, and the consequences of clientelism, about which I wrote in the 1970s. This is because of an authoritarian administrative system that never saw the citizen in the French republican sense of being an equal. It was because the relationship of the citizen with the State system was devalued.

There is a communicative power where there is no connection between the vulnerability, the struggle and the agony of ordinary people at this time, and the description of what is news, of what is happening in the world which they inhabit. They do not have equal access to the story; rather, it is for those who work in the sector. I was Minister with responsibility for broadcast communications. This is not an Irish phenomenon. Across Europe and the Western World, people will say that they must be cynical about presenting what the viewing or listening public will accept as the news of the day. This kind of artificial connection between what is moral and what is ethical is incredibly dangerous.

It is widening an excluded underclass in Ireland. It is creating people who will move quickly to conflict because there are no mediating institutions in Europe. In one country after another across Africa and Asia, as people overthrow dictatorships, they place their trust first in representative institutions and then, if they are let down, they are into a straight conflict with what are regarded as the forces of law and order. The result is war, and the waste of human and other resources in the terrible tasks of war.

I say this not to depress anybody but simply to state that since I was a child in County Clare I have had a belief in the power of education and in the power of ideas. However, I believe that an enormously high price has been paid for a kind of anti-intellectualism and authoritarianism in Irish culture. Therefore, I believe that we need to draw one conclusion. We need not suggest that that which has failed us should, or can be, repaired. This is why the Labour Party is incredibly important in leading a government. We need to go back and recover the promise of a real republic that would be built on citizenship and that would reject as outrageous in a republic the kind of radical individualism epitomised in that ugly statement of Michael McDowell's that inequality is needed for the stability of society. It ranks with Margaret Thatcher's view that there is no such thing as society. It stands there as such a notion. People should have seen immediately how incongruous it was to speak like this with a hubris drawn from the language of radical individualism.

Instead of speaking about the republic that might be created, people spoke about 'getting a bit of the action'. Suddenly it was no longer important to have just one house for shelter, or to have another for pension purposes, in case a family split up or somebody retired. One needed a string of houses – and thus our property bubble was created, within a bubble of speculative capitalism that had flowed from an attack on the Glass-Steagall Act of 1933 in the United States, which had introduced regulations following the Great Crash. President Clinton gave in after several years of lobbying by those who stated that it was necessary to get rid of all the regulations so that the instruments needed by the market could be pushed out to absorb what was regarded as an endless flow of credit. What was this? It was an irrational form of capitalism, and thus one of the projects now is the idea of whether capitalism can save itself again.

I believe that as Ireland moves into a time when we can celebrate the founding of my party, the great Lockout, and the 1916 Rising, we need to think about an entirely different kind of society. I am immensely practical about this. I can suggest – I have spoken and I have written elsewhere and will continue to do so – that what one would do if one wanted to deliver what I am describing in terms of political participation, administrative fairness and the equality of the right to communicate, would be to speak about a floor of citizenship below which people would not be allowed to fall. One would make people secure from the time of birth to very old age – when at the moment they wonder whether they will have to leave their homes to die, as they frequently do within eighteen months of being sent to a nursing home. One would make it possible that children share the same class, and for that period of their lives at least would be able to be equal with regard to education. In addition to this, people would have decent housing.

This was the agenda when Sean O'Casey wrote about disparity. James Connolly took the Irish Citizen Army, with its egalitarian agenda, and placed it side by side with nationalism. The lesson we learned from this was that when the egalitarian socialist agenda was placed side by side with the nationalist agenda, it would be the socialist agenda which would lose. This was in the dialogue immediately before the meeting of the First Dáil, when Michael Collins told the IRB it need not be too bothered with the content of the Democratic Programme, because they were just going through with it to keep Labour onside.

Those of us in favour of a version of Ireland where no one will fall below a certain level of security in social and economic terms must say it not only to ourselves but also to Europe. In addition, a highly participative, inclusive republic was the one in the vision of those who made the case for Irish independence at the end of the nineteenth century and the beginning of the twentieth century. It was this which was stolen from the people after the foundation of the State, when the conservatives marched into all the principal professorships, including education and philosophy. UCD became a stable for conservatism, and suddenly one had the continuation of an administrative nightmare and the robbing of the people of the delivery of the republic with regard to their ordinary lives.

Frequently, people such as the Slovenian philosopher Slavoj Žižek, currently in favour with the extreme Left in Europe, have said to me that if things are as I describe them, then what is needed is a form of terror that would sweep everything away, and enable us to start all over again. A terrible price would of course have to be paid for this, so therefore one must put one's faith in representative democracy – and having done so, one wants it to work. If one wants it to work, one must be open to transformation, to making the type of institutional changes that can deliver a real alternative. How could this be carried through? There is need, as a beginning, for a discourse in which we are able to speak about the vulnerabilities that matter, and where there is not a huge gulf between what we say in here and what is happening on the street.

People wonder why poverty has to reproduce itself in the same family from one generation to another, or from one area to another, and wonder why there is a difference between the quality of schools in one place and the quality of those in another. God did not make it like that. Nature did not make it like that. The people in the so-called Irish republic made it like that, and they maintained it like that. I remember in County Clare when one could point to the two or three people in the Labour Party because they lived in a galvanised house. People would explain that they were Labour in the same way as they would say they were on the margins of society – and they were. Therefore, with regard to thinking that the Finance Bill is necessary for this, that or the other, I hope the new government realises that the model, which is broken, should not be repaired, and that there is a discourse now which is wider and which is not only in Ireland but in Europe, where citizens are wondering what institutions might best express that which we wish to share with each other, where the concept of interdependency is accepted, and where it would be regarded as obscene to state that radical individualism is what is important and what must drive us. All that radical individualism, with its privileged view of professions and its side-of-the-mouth politics with regard to benefit and privilege, is what must be rejected.

This has a practical expression in Europe. If we create here a radical, inclusive republic, we will place it in a social Europe which accepts the interdependency of peoples rather than the aspirations of the elite property-owning classes and individual countries. We would then be able to be a region in the global sense, which offered guarantees about labour, security and peace. It would be a powerful moral voice in the world with regard to having alternatives to war and allowing people to initiate and follow their own paths to development, which would be very attractive.

With regard to the Bill, the question the people ask, which the new government must address, is *Why?* The new government must speak endlessly about jobs. This is the point for people who lose their jobs or are told that they must be made unemployed. Everyone here is very reasonable, and I ask people to be at least accurate about one thing I remember in this House, which is the night in September 2008 when the Labour Party was left alone. The vote was 129 votes to 18 votes. We were the 18. We voted, and sustained debate through two nights, with regard to an unlimited guarantee that joined the debts of our speculative banks to the deficit issues of the economy. This is what we are facing tonight.

I also say this now looking forward: I hope the discourse we will have now will speak about inclusion. This Bill contains some good things, but there are ridiculous ones. I will give one example of what I meant by the phrases 'political power' and 'administrative power'. In my long time in here, people agitated, for example, for the equality legislation that was introduced by my colleague Mervyn Taylor. People imagined that when we had got the equality legislation, we had arrived at a particular point, but the political science would have indicated that this political power was useless without administrative power. It was only when the equality legislation was followed through with the Equality Authority and the Combat Poverty Agency that it was possible to administer the benefit that had been won politically. That is the meaning of administrative power – and is why we lost the Combat Poverty Agency and the Equality Agency to the Right, and had all the cuts. That is what citizens in a republic want: they want more political power and more administrative power. They want to communicate their vulnerability and want to be able to respond to each other's interdependency. The very last thing they want is more of the same, conveyed in such language as that terrible saying 'We are where we are'. Such language is what has brought us to this point now. That is why I am proud to be president of the Labour Party. If we have failed from time to time, what has never been in doubt is that we were speaking about a real republic that has yet to be built in this State.

Speaking on the Second Stage of the Finance Bill,
26 March 2011

2.

Transforming Ireland, 2011–2016: The Role of Uachtarán na hÉireann

That Ireland is in need of transformation no one can now doubt.

Owing to the actions of those in whom trust was placed, be it by commission or omission, we have lost much of our economic sovereignty and independence. Our international reputation has also been damaged. Yet within Ireland powerful capacities, great intelligence and talent remain, capable of acknowledging and rejecting that which has failed, and, even more importantly, capable of recognising those principles upon which our shared future must now be built.

This transformation must be one that deepens engagement rather then bowing to cynicism – that extends rather than erodes democracy – and that initiates changes not just in our political structures, but also in our institutions, our language, our way of dealing with each other, and in our consciousness.

It is my conviction that a certain version of Ireland which prevailed in our recent past must now be regarded as over and rejected. That narrow version of Ireland was not based on the best of our traditions, nor drawn from the true potential of the contemporary period. Rather it was characterised by an extreme and unrestrained individualism and an almost reverential approach to wealth and speculation that too often pushed social concerns to the margins. There was a real disconnect between an irresponsible elite and the ongoing struggles of many citizens who found themselves excluded.

This version of Irish society was destructive at home, and it damaged our reputation abroad. In Europe and elsewhere, indeed, some commentators were astounded at the unrestrained arrogance of some of our spokespersons.

It must then be a starting point, in the transformation that we need, that we recognise that there should be no going back to that inadequate and unworthy version of ourselves.

Yet Ireland must also now, I believe, move beyond recrimination and beyond cynicism, and draw on our strengths and on the very best aspects of ourselves – our generous humanity, our humour, our rich heritage and our creativity – to create something new, emancipatory and transformative. I believe that the presidency has a powerful contribution to make to this transformation.

As someone who in another role, as a political scientist, taught in this area, I am very aware of the potential and indeed the limitations of the office of the president.

The presidency has essentially three main functions. It has a constitutional role and a ceremonial role, both of which must be conducted with dignity and sophistication, recognising that one is speaking not just for oneself but for all the Irish people. The third area is where the character of the presidency is defined: the discretionary area available to the president. How it is used in terms of choice of themes addressed, whom you speak to, and when, are matters of great importance, as was demonstrated in the previous presidencies. It is these discretionary choices that define the values that are lodged in the incumbent's interpretation of the office.

The president cannot be an organising point of opposition to the government of the day – but has the capacity to address important issues that are far wider in theme and time.

The affirmation that the president of Ireland makes on taking office states: 'I will dedicate my abilities to the service and welfare of the people of Ireland.' In Irish it is even stronger: '*Mo lándicheall a dhéanamh ar son leasa is fónaimh mhuintir na hÉireann.*'

These words are a powerful mandate, a great challenge – and part of what inspired me to seek the presidency.

As a candidate for president, I offer a vision of a radically inclusive citizenship, in a creative society, worthy of a real republic – making us proud to be Irish in the world.

My candidacy, and this vision, are underpinned by years of service to the public at every level, from councillor to Cabinet minister to president of the European Council of Culture Ministers. My participation in public life has always been characterised by a genuine independence of mind and a strong policy-driven emphasis in everything I have done.

In deciding last year to seek a nomination for the presidency, I deliberately announced the decision early. Rather then return to the Dáil last February, I decided, out of respect for the constituents I had represented for twenty-five years, and as a mark of my commitment to this new and important challenge, to step aside and devote myself entirely and uncompromisingly to the campaign to become president of Ireland: an honour, and an opportunity, which I take very seriously.

Returning to the four important and deeply interconnected aspects of Ireland's transformation which I have proposed in my vision for the presidency – an inclusive citizenship, a creative society, a real republic, and pride in being Irish in the world – I believe that Uachtarán na hÉireann has both an inspirational and a practical role to play in each of these areas.

A Real Republic

I believe that, in many senses, the republic of equals which was sought, and which inspired so many who took part in the 1913 Lockout, the Easter Rising and the War of Independence, has never been fully realised. It has, however, stayed alive as an ideal and has re-emerged in movements for social justice and equality throughout the years, and in campaigns for participation and inclusion.

The time has now come to reassert that sense of possibility and to turn our collective efforts to the creation of a real republic. That real republic has to be based on a recognition of the dignity of every citizen, irrespective of gender, capacity, orientation or means. It is that recognition of dignity which is the common principle across all cultures where there is a meaningful pursuit of human rights.

If elected president of Ireland, I will support those initiatives where citizens are again actively imagining and debating our shared vision as a nation. I will also take a strong interest in the deliberations and outcomes of the National Constitutional Convention proposed by the government.

I would further hope to enhance such processes of interrogation and renewal by becoming patron to a series of Presidency Seminars, inviting participation from a wide cross-section of society and addressing wider issues, such as the restoration of trust in our institutions, participation and inclusion within our communities, Ireland's role in developing a more generous social European project, our relationship with the environment, deepening connections with those who have left, and issues of global interdependency.

Inclusive Citizenship

In recent years, in my book *Causes for Concern*, and in a number of papers, I have been consistently calling for a meaningful debate on citizenship – a real debate which, while it would include the generosity that is involved in volunteering, would go much further and also debate an appropriate rights base for citizenship.

I believe we must now promote a positive vision of what it means to be a citizen in Ireland. This citizenship should be based on equality and respect, with a basic level of rights and participation – a citizenship floor – below which no one should be allowed to fall. We need to move away from radical individualism towards a radical kind of inclusion.

Inclusion means valuing diversity in all its forms and challenging exclusion wherever it occurs. No one in our society should experience the destructive effects of discrimination, isolation or rejection.

Inclusion means celebrating solidarity by recognising the aspirations, concerns, creativity and potential of every citizen, regardless of their age, orientation, capacities or means. Inclusive citizenship also brings shared responsibility – a life that goes beyond the self to include those around us and, indeed, the generations yet to come.

If elected president, I will use the discretion that the office allows to highlight initiatives for inclusion across Ireland and actively to promote a citizenship based on equality, respect, solidarity and participation.

The Creative Society

In terms of Ireland's reputation, one of our greatest strengths, constantly renewed, has been the acknowledged creativity of Irish people. This is a powerful resource in the reconstruction of a better version of ourselves both at home and abroad.

Ireland has produced, and continues to produce, wonderful writers, artists, playwrights, poets and musicians – yet such artists are only one example of what can be possible in a creative society in which each citizen is given the opportunity to imagine and contribute. The creative society cannot be imposed from above; it is built on creativity made possible in communities. Properly respected, the cultural space can be an invitation to push the boundaries of the possible – enfranchising us all in our capacity for living, and enriching the social and economic life of the nation.

As Ireland's first Minister for the Arts, Culture and the Gaeltacht, I saw the transformative potential of creativity – a potential I helped realise by means of practical measures such as the redevelopment of the Irish film industry; the setting up of Teilifís na Gaeilge, now TG4; the removal of Section 31 of the Broadcasting Acts, so that the voices of all could be heard by all; the establishment of a network of local arts and cultural venues throughout the State; but also by seeking to forge a different kind of national relationship with the arts, moving them from the margins of society to the very centre of our economic and social development.

I saw the potential of creativity then, and see it even more clearly today. Creativity is not limited to the artistic, or aesthetic, aspects of our lives. The real republic of which I speak is one that is creative in research; creative in innovation and tradition; creative in how we do business; creative in its supports for and celebration of young people and older people; creative in peacemaking, diplomacy and international development; creative in sport and dance; creative in multilingualism and in our use of our own language; creative in our relationship with our diaspora and with those who have joined us in Ireland, particularly in recent years; creative in how we speak to each other, in how we relate to one another and to our environment.

There is rich potential, as I recognised as minister and see still today, in the creative industries – seedbeds of innovation and collaboration which can offer rich rewards in the creation of new jobs at the local and national level and in strengthening Ireland's part in the knowledge economy. Indeed, creativity is the vital ingredient in such economic activities as software development, the creation and development of new electronic games for a vast world market, animation, film, studio production, and indeed the audiovisual and film industry, whose value grew from €11 million at the beginning of my time as minister to €187 million at its end, and is now estimated at over €500 million.

However, such creative industries can only flourish in a sustainable way if they are rooted in creative communities where every child and adult has the opportunity to contribute and imagine and where there is access to the cultural and creative spaces for all citizens. The creative society invites us to challenge the boundaries of the inevitable and open up to new possibilities, to the suggestions of the heart as well as the head, or even more importantly, to avoid the unnecessary choice between them.

Ireland, and Being Irish in the World

The president is Ireland's face to the outside world, and should draw on the best traditions on which our international reputation is built. This includes excellence in culture and the arts, creativity in business, pride in our heritage, respect earned through our record in humanitarian work and in peacekeeping, and the important contributions and connections made by our diaspora in so many countries.

A priority of my presidency will be to strengthen and deepen all strands of our international reputation. I believe that being Irish in the world is something we should all be proud of.

Another priority will be the strengthening of Ireland's connection with its wide diaspora. As far back as 1969, I began research on the subject of emigration, and I have retained a burning interest in the fate of our emigrants and the role of our diaspora since then. My sisters emigrated to Manchester as young women and my nephews and nieces live in England. My uncle and aunt from my father's family are buried in Australia. As a sociologist, I actually ran the first course on the sociology of emigration in this country. In fact, the early papers I gave to the Patrick MacGill Summer School were on the topic of emigration and how it had informed writings such as that of Patrick MacGill, Peadar O'Donnell and Donall Mac Amhalaigh. I also contributed over the years to a number of Dáil and Oireachtas Committee debates on this subject, urging the establishment of effective support structures for the Irish in Britain, and seeking to change and regularise the status of the undocumented Irish in the United States. It has been my practice in recent years to visit Irish Centres in Britain regularly to demonstrate my interest in, and solidarity with, the Irish there. As president of the Labour Party, I am particularly proud of the fact that it was Ruairi Quinn, as Minister in 1984, who introduced the State Committee *Díon*, as the first ever grant-giving agency to aid and assist emigrant voluntary care agencies abroad.

As president, I would wish to reach out to all sections and all generations of the Irish abroad, particularly those young people who have recently left. Wherever they make their new lives, be it Manchester, Toronto, Beijing or Buenos Aires, we must, I believe, emphasise to them the important role that they can still play, even while abroad, in contributing to the cultural, economic and social fabric of Ireland – inviting them to maintain their connection with Ireland, celebrate their Irishness, and play some part in our national recovery. In this regard, the building of stronger Irish networks in all countries where the Irish assemble is of critical importance.

As president, I would hope to be patron of these emerging networks, which should serve not only as valuable and necessary support mechanisms for the Irish within those countries, but also as business-related networks which could, over time, promote new employment projects in Ireland and strengthen access to international markets for Irish companies, including in emerging economies such as China, India and Brazil.

Representing ourselves abroad in our best sense means celebrating all that makes Ireland unique, and in that sense I will also be proud to promote the Irish language as a living, vibrant and beautifully expressive language.

Returning then to the theme of this summer school: transformation. I believe that the transformation we need must be rooted in the best instincts of both the head and the heart. It is something that can never be delivered by cold market economics alone.

Over the years, most of the genuinely progressive changes we have seen in Ireland have been made possible by those who followed that generous and courageous instinct of the heart which tells us to reach out to others and to respect their essential dignity.

I have been proud to be part of many of those struggles for civil and political rights, including a rights-based approach to disability, the rights of women and children, and those discriminated against on the basis of sexual orientation. I have been proud also to have helped drive change on issues such as the ending of the status of the illegitimacy of children, divorce, same-sex unions, access to contraception, equality of opportunity and equal pay.

There were times too when a price had to be paid for transformation – as when the pursuit of political principle and a genuine independence of mind led to the loss of seats for the late Jim Kemmy and myself in the 1980s.

The same values, the same commitment that have consistently underpinned my work for justice and equality at home and abroad over the last thirty years, now inform this vision I have offered for Ireland's next presidency.

In summary, I offer a record of principle and practice and a vision for Ireland based on clear values of inclusion, respect, creativity and solidarity. I believe that the knowledge and experience I have gained at every level of Irish society, and in representing Ireland abroad, will be of immense benefit to me as president.

Connolly spoke of the importance of employing whatever 'gifts of hand or brain one has, to deliver for one's fellow citizens'. In seeking to take up that challenge in the office of president, I offer both head and heart.

As a child growing up in Clare, I knew poverty and loss. But it was years later, as the first member of my family to go to college, that I found the ideas that matched the instinct for equality which I felt in my heart. That is why I have always sought to share these ideas with my fellow citizens, and why I set them out in this vision for our presidency and our future. In a republic, there should be no idea in any area of our life lived together, whether in politics, economy or society, that is considered beyond the reach of a citizen.

Ideas and creativity are two of the most democratic and transformative forces we have, and they belong to all equally. Recently, I have been travelling right across the country, and I have drawn inspiration from that very active nine months of engaging with, and listening to, people throughout Ireland. Everywhere I go I meet citizens who want to talk about ideas, who are tired of being underestimated – young people in particular who want to play their part in a real republic.

I believe that our country is full of potential. I believe that there are traditional decencies which remain very strong. I believe that the country is peopled with imaginative, creative citizens, with unlimited potential and possibility, and that the role of the president is to be an inspiration and support to this new Ireland, which we are all called to build. It is a time to play to our strengths, to enhance our reputation.

I believe that Ireland can, and must, emerge from this present crisis with a more responsible model of economy and state, and with engaged citizens who will, together, ensure that the mistakes of the past are not repeated. In the future, we may be proud to remember how, together, we built something real out of the worst of times, something both visionary and practical.

I am more than ready to undertake a vigorous campaign to faithfully serve the people of Ireland as a president of courage, integrity and vision for the next seven years.

Delivered at the MacGill Summer School,
29 July 2011

3.

Of Solidarity and Citizenship

As we are all aware, May Day has long been synonomous with International Workers' Day, or Labour Day. Rooted in the struggle of workers, the commemoration of May Day has been with us ever since 1889, as a celebration of the social and economic achievements of the labour movement across the globe.

As president of the Labour Party, I am particularly proud of the role which our party has played in defending and improving the rights of Irish workers since its establishment in 1912 by James Connolly, James Larkin and William O'Brien, as the political wing of the Irish Trade Union Congress. Under the leadership of Tom Johnson TD, Labour brought constitutional politics to Ireland by providing the Opposition in the Dáil after the opponents of the Treaty left and precipitated the Civil War. Our leader, Tom Johnson TD, was also the author of the programme for the First Dáil.

The Labour Party is the oldest party in Ireland and was founded in the year before one of the greatest confrontations between labour and capital in the history of the Irish state: the great Lockout in Dublin of 1913.

What was then a poverty-stricken, and vulnerable, movement

of labour sought to organise against a version of capitalism that refused the most basic rights to workers, including the very right to organise. That confrontation required courage, tenacity, solidarity and, above all, a commitment to class and history beyond the short-term challenges. We should never forget that, to this day, we are the beneficiaries of the struggle of the labour movement of 1913. Moreover, as their heirs, we are required to make an analysis of our own difficult times, to craft a strategy, and to deliver our view of an alternative society with a sustainable and productive connection between economy and society, and institutions that can deliver it.

Today, the Labour Party, under the inspired leadership of Tánaiste Eamon Gilmore TD, and with the highest number of Teachtai Dála and senators in our party's history, is central to the solutions which need to be devised, and will be devised, to restore our country's economy, to create jobs for our workforce, to protect the vulnerable and less fortunate in our society, and also to restore Ireland's once-proud international reputation.

But, also today, the Labour Party is at the cusp of taking one of its most important decisions on its future centrality of place in the body politic, and in ensuring that the significant gains of the past can be not only consolidated but also brought into the main-stream, and secured for the future. Now that the Seanad elections are over, the new Labour Party Parliamentary Party, along with the National Executive, will meet within weeks to select the party's can-didate for the elections in October for President of Ireland. Labour is now uniquely placed to achieve the goal of a Labour Party President, who would be in place to commemorate such important anniversaries as the 1912 foundation of our party, the 1913 Lockout, and the Easter Rising of 1916. What better culmination of the gains of the past could that achievement signal for those many of us who have been promoting Labour Party values with conviction and passion throughout our lives?

I believe that, by selecting me as the party's candidate for the election, Labour can, and will be, successful in the presidential elections. I believe that the party will be best served by putting me forward, and I would like to take this opportunity to offer some of the reasons why I believe this to be the case.

I believe that it is time to move beyond recrimination and, especially, to move beyond the corrosive individualism of recent years, which has caused so much economic and social upheaval to our country and its citizens. At the same time, that which has failed must not be repaired. It is time for a period of active citizenship, intergenerational solidarity, and the rebuilding of trust, linked to a new engagement with our rich diaspora, which will be built on a reconnection with Ireland and the delivery of tangible benefits for Ireland.

What experience would I bring to the Office of President of Ireland?

Since the time when I first stood for election in 1969, I have dedicated my life to politics and to public life, and I have a proven record in the promotion of equality of opportunity between women and men in our society; in protecting the vulnerable, the less fortunate and the disabled in our society; and in defending human rights and fundamental freedoms across the globe, in recognition of the dignity of all human beings and in rejection of power elites who abuse that power and undermine that dignity.

I have been a local and national politician throughout my adult life, and have had the honour to be a member of Dáil Éireann for twenty-five years and of Seanad Éireann for a further nine years. I have also served as Ireland's first ever Minister for the Arts, and as a full Cabinet Minister for five years, listing as my more significant achievements during that period the repeal of Section 31 of the Broadcasting Act, which had a seminal impact on the then-emerging peace process for our island; the promotion of our national language; and in particular the establishment of Teilifís na Gaeilge, now TG4, as well as the creation of jobs and the promotion of economic development in our Gaeltachtaí; the re-establishment of the Irish film industry, thus providing essential access for our actors, producers, designers, musicians and technicians; the funding of a rich network of arts and cultural venues throughout the State, which are exciting the imagination and skills of our citizens to this day; and the revitalisation of our waterways network, including the promotion of cross-border commerce and leisure activities via the opening of the Shannon-Erne Waterway, an important precursor to the rich tapestry of cross-border connectivity which we enjoy today.

At the European level, I served as president of the EU's Council of Culture Ministers and on the EU's Council of Broadcasting Ministers for a period of six months, and brought a distinct Irish dimension to the deliberations of these two councils. I have also served at local level, including two terms as Mayor of Galway and many years on Galway County Council and Galway City Council.

While my roots are firmly embedded in rural Ireland – I was born in Limerick and educated in Clare – I have lived much of my life in Galway city with my wife Sabina and my four children. I have experienced all the ups and downs, the challenges and the struggles, of our economy and society throughout that period, and it is that experience which, I believe, will enable me to foster a new, warmly empathetic, and constructive engagement with the people of Ireland as their president. That experience will, however, also allow me to build a new engagement with the government of the day, and, with changing institutions and structures, the alternative society which I have often referred to, and which must emerge in the next few years as we face the significant challenges which Ireland must overcome.

As part of a lifelong commitment to human rights, I have highlighted, campaigned in, and in many cases travelled to areas of conflict in many parts of the world, including Nicaragua, Turkey, Western Sahara, Chile, Gaza, the West Bank, Peru, El Salvador, Iraq and Somalia. In recognition of my persistent promotion of peace with justice, I became the first recipient of the Seán MacBride Peace Prize of the International Peace Bureau in Helsinki in 1992.

I also have a strong record in the academic world as both a lecturer and contributor to many international journals on the subjects of political science, political economy and sociology. I am currently Adjunct Professor on Human Rights at the Irish Centre for Human Rights at the National University of Ireland, Galway.

I should also emphasise that my lifetime commitment to, and connection with, the Irish language is not based on any superficial interest in the language. Rather, is it based on my firm belief that our language is a repository of the national memory and an essential connection with those who have passed before us on this island.

What values would I bring to the Office of President of Ireland?

I believe that the injustices that motivated the founders of the Labour Party – poverty, inequality, the exploitation of vulnerable workers, the trampling on the rights of women and children, inadequate access to education and health care – though not as brutal as when Labour was founded, do still remain. This is particularly ironic following a period of unprecedented opportunity in terms of the availability of capital and current funds – funds that could, and should, have been used to transform Ireland, providing a floor of social protection and enabling significant gains to be made towards achieving an equality of citizenship within the republic.

I believe that the pernicious and self-interested individualism without restraint, inspired and promoted by Thatcherism and Reaganism, and by recent Irish governments, has led to a de-peopled system and has undermined the solidarity which is essential for our society. There is a need in Ireland for a radical, inclusive society that regards citizenship as being built on equality, as valuing solidarity and as being rooted in caring.

Within that radical inclusive society, there is also a need for a strong inter-generational solidarity which recognises the aspirations and concerns of all age-groups and taps the skills and resources of all those groups in meeting the significant challenges which lie ahead.

In the absence of a radical inclusive society, it follows that I believe that we have yet to engage in the task of establishing what I would describe as a real republic. After the War of Independence, there was an almost seamless institutional continuity which ran on from many of the British institutions, with not-dissimilar degrees of privilege, patriarchy and hierarchy. In effect, many of those who fought for independence and were inspired by the laudable ideals of the 1916 Proclamation had their version of a Republic stolen from them.

We now urgently need to work together to create the foundations of a real republic, based on the needs, aspirations, imagination and genius of all our people in their different ways. In a real republic, the right to shelter, food security, education, a good and sustainable environment, and freedom from fear and insecurity, from childhood to old age, must be the benchmarks. Indeed, I have long advocated this concept of a 'citizenship floor' – a minimum set of rights which are non-negotiable and must be provided for all citizens.

We must now build a new citizenship, for which we need a new discourse. That is the only true basis of a real solidarity. This new citizenship must be an active and participative citizenship, where the views of all sections of society are given appropriate voice, and where the institutions of the State respond to those views by developing an alternative and responsible model of our economy. We must insist on an Ireland where participation is based on citizenship and rights, rather than on the wealth that one possesses. I am also anxious to emphasise that, in a real republic, the concept of citizenship also requires an acceptance of obligations and duties, as well as rights – in effect, a life beyond the self.

We must build a creative society which recognises and values the cultural space as independent from the economic space. Properly respected, this cultural space can be not merely a location for the arts but a source of vision, offering innovation in our capacity for living, including economic life, and a necessary defining capacity for our quality of life. Our cultural space, however, must above all other considerations constitute a building block in our citizenship.

The creative industries have a very real contribution to make to economic wealth and employment in Ireland. Moreover, the multiplier effect from such economic activities is substantial, and sustainable, and has the potential to make a wide-reaching impact right across Ireland.

The creativity and cultural content evident in areas such as craft, clothing, furniture and indeed food can also make a crucial contribution to our success. Factory floors are in some cases being replaced by creative communities whose raw material is their ability to imagine, create and innovate.

Apart from its impact on employment and growth, culture can of course prevent and treat some of the emerging tensions of our society; it can help build an understanding of the many facets of sustainability; it can bring about a new sense of solidarity; it can positively inspire the new economy; and, in particular, it can act as a means of empowerment and entitlement.

Ireland's cultural players have demonstrated these aspects of our culture admirably and consistently. They have put genius into the version of Ireland they have delivered abroad and, if the people bestow the honour on me to become president, my overriding objective will be to represent Ireland in its reputational best sense.

There is now an urgent need to promote serious, informed public debate and to demonstrate courageous leadership in response to the dilution of trust which has so clearly taken place in all Ireland's traditional 'institutions', whether they be politics and politicians, the Church, the banks, the professions, our hospitals, or the media. I believe that this contagion of distrust can have a corrosive effect on the hopes and aspirations of all of us, and that every strand of civil society must now combine and create space for courageous leadership, backed up by efficient and effective institutions and structures. The contribution of Ireland's large diaspora to meeting the significant challenges which lie ahead must also be addressed.

1 May 2011

4.

Building the Politics of a Real Republic

Labour, and indeed Ireland, stand today at an intersection, a defining point, in political, social and economic terms. The society is regarded by many as post-ethical in character. Economic growth has not been utilised to reduce inequality or achieve universal provision and an effective delivery of services. We are now into a new century, which has so far, sadly, been marked less by an egalitarian impulse than the last century – indeed, it is characterised by the erosion of many hard-won rights of citizens.

Despite regular government trumpeting of the contribution of social partnership to growth, the rights to which I refer – the right to organise, the right of collective bargaining, issues pertaining to workers' rights (rights that are fundamental, as is the importance of preventing the exploitation of workers) – are being undermined.

Labour stands for, and will continue to campaign for, a truly universalist approach to human rights both at home and abroad. These are battles to which our party was at the forefront and on which it must continue to give a lead. Before the general election, we in Labour pledged to ratify the Convention on the Protection of all Migrant Workers and their Families during the election campaign. This remains our policy.

Much of the energies of the Labour movement since our foundation in 1912 to the present moment have concentrated on the protection of workers in a hostile environment. These protections have had to be won through negotiation, but often, too, through courageous confrontation.

In the period into which we have now entered, it is clear that this task remains. Many commentators, often with vested interests and barely veiled motives, argue that there is no need for strong union representation, for example. They say that we have reached a stage where such concerns are beneath us.

They could not be more wrong. And while we are plotting the future for our party – a task that Conference will debate – it is imperative that while we modernise and renew our party, we also take from that which was the best of our past. We in the Labour Party, while respecting the complexity of the real circumstances of the economy and the society in which we find ourselves, are not required to capitulate to the version of the economy or the society which those on the Right are suggesting is inevitable.

The debate to which we must contribute is not merely a national one. It is also both European and global. In the forthcoming debate on the European Treaty, for example, we must stress the need for 'social Europe' to become a reality. We must defeat the attempt to relegate the aim of cohesion to the status of a pious afterthought to an unrestricted competition. In the name of alleged labour-market flexibility, and an appeal for competitiveness in the world's most unregulated and exploitative labour markets, hard-won securities for workers have been challenged, and those who are most vulnerable are those without trade union representation.

In one of the composite motions before us this weekend – and one which I am proud to say emanated from one of the branches in Galway West, my constituency – we are asked to consider the particular difficulties experienced by those employed in the private sector who are without the right to trade union representation, and calls for the implementation of the legislation passed by Dáil Éireann so as to give the full force of law in the State to the EU Employment Directive on Information and Consultation Framework by establishing and resourcing a proper inspectorate. The motion goes on to call on the government to implement the legislation so as to provide agency workers with the same terms and conditions of employment as are enjoyed by full-time employees.

It is with this kind of principled thinking and action that we can begin to make our mark on this new Dáil term, and in shaping this young century. This is the sort of issue which can portray Labour at its best: a campaigning party committed to freedom and equality, certainly to helping the under-represented and the voiceless, but also to the building of a different society.

The rewards of a campaigning commitment have been in evidence over the past number of years also. Be it in our strong Bills on civil unions, on collective representation, on public transport, education and health, or an enhanced level of overseas development aid provision – that is the kind of campaigning work we need to do, and to continue to do. It is what is needed in the public space.

We must now begin to chart a course for the future. We must analyse the general election of last May, and extrapolate from the results.

I believe that there is a great hunger, not just among young people but generally in society, for a politics that seeks little less than the radical recovery of the public world, for the rebuilding of a basis of trust, and for the reconstitution of the social bond in such a way as would give real meaning to an inclusive citizenship. This will require, however, making a political choice in policies between what is good, indeed necessary, for the citizenry as a whole, and what is being sought for the advancement, in a totally uncontrolled way, of such private interests as undermine the very basis of society. Can we affect a neutrality in the face of such actions as the surrendering or the loss of spaces and properties accumulated for public services, and their transfer through forms of alleged public/private partnership for private gain? Obviously not, is the answer.

On the grounds of public hospitals, sites are handed over to for-profit private investors. In Galway, at Ceannt Station, land accumulated for public transport is offered to attract the minimal capital amounts for public transport, and that might well have been included in the government's capital programme. Indeed, as regards the public space itself, and the very right to be in the street, it has been Labour, in my own city of Galway, that has run the successful campaigns for the right to assemble and to distribute literature in the public street. It is not an exaggeration to say that from the streets to the foreshore, there is no public space that is not under threat from speculative predators with straightforward connections to the government parties, and, scandalously, with parts of the public administrative system.

The connections between the economy, the society and the administrative system are inescapably political, and Labour's view of these connections is the very opposite of what currently prevails. We stand for an economy that is accountable and transparent in terms of the social goals it serves. We stand for social goals that have been established and have received a mandate from the people. Just think of how different this is from a version of government where a Taoiseach reappoints a Minister for Health whose party has been comprehensively rejected in a general election. With her appointment, the Taoiseach has chosen to inflict a rejected model of privatised medicine on public sites on the people without any mandate.

To give meaning to a politics capable of addressing the issues of our time, we need, I repeat, to have a debate on the relationships, and the assumptions that connect the society and the economy.

Since Ireland began its transformation to one of the world's richest countries, public debate has tended to centre on the economy, particularly its transformation since the 1990s, when growth, sustained by exports, began, and continued after 2000 without such an export performance but rather based on a revaluation of the property base of the society.

During the years of the Celtic Tiger economic boom, and indeed even now, well into the twenty-first century, talk at all levels of Irish society frequently centres on economic growth. Great pride is – rightly – taken in the rapid climb we made in our development as a nation, which was in such stark contrast to some previous decades. Because of these recent developments, concerns about our economic output have centred on the need to prevent the economy 'overheating', and undoing what is regarded as the good work which had been achieved. Issues of income distribution are rarely given a central emphasis.

Beyond such a concentration, however, there are more crucial questions, some of which we share with other countries in the European Union. More and more, we are being driven, rather than choosing, to ask questions as to the nature of the connection between the economy and the society. These have included more than the obvious, if neglected, basic questions as to the equitable distribution of wealth or the fairness of taxation. They have raised fundamental questions as to the degree to which a general inclusion and a full participation has been made possible for our citizens. Indeed, we have been forced to question the means by which we might remain both citizens and consumers. Some commentators have gone so far as to suggest that we have begun a process of being consumed in our consumption, of being less a society than a volatile and insatiable market.

What does it mean to be an Irish citizen? Simple critiques of what is perceived to be the materialistic implications of increased and complex consumption are insufficient. An agenda for living requires us to seek to specify the realms of economics and to define the social and cultural spaces as being wider than the economic space. Refusing to accept such a proposition is seriously to limit citizenship.

Culture, beyond all the definitional difficulties, is based on what we share, the assumptions as to what we regard as inevitable, the ideas by which we live, or the uncritical existence through which we drift in conditions of unfreedom. It is a process that is continually being reworked. Because our values are shared, they constitute the bedrock of the public world – a public world that is under threat from the demands of a privatised world, predicated on consumption, and the protection of which is often based on a fear of others. 'The other' is less an equal citizen than a potential begrudger. Thus the shared trust of citizens in the public space is replaced by the insecurity of private possessions.

It is important to recognise the political implications of accepting the alternative: the hegemony of the social and the cultural space over the economic. A neo-liberal model that is over-reliant on market provision cannot produce a space of citizenship, a public space, a truly public world. Indeed, it tends to destroy it, colonising, as it were, the public space of citizenship with the private demands of consumption.

There is now, then, a real need for Labour members to emphasise that there is more than one version of an economic order, and that which currently dominates in Ireland or Europe is by no means the only one. Neither is it the most efficient or effective version. Labour members must realise that the making of the case for an

41

alternative depends on themselves. A servile, monopolised media will always choose the vicarious rather than the critical.

This economy might be referred to as a 'de-peopled economy'. What does this mean? What it means is that all is predicated on the needs and demands of the economic, at the expense of all else. We do not work to live; rather, in too many examples, we live to work. At the top, of course, it is assumed that it will take millions to induce a director of a bank to open the curtains in the morning. John Maynard Keynes wrote in his day of what he called the 'immoral ratio of difference' between the top and the average earner, if it reached 50 to 1. Today a ratio of 500 to 1 results in media admiration in Ireland.

Too much else of our potential life experience is either denied us, or is seriously curtailed. In essence, issues pertaining to family, community and society are all too often superseded by an imposed devotion to maintaining the economy. But it goes much further than that. Across the dimensions of space and time, we are forced, be it in terms of enforced limitations in housing or, in the absence of public transport, to huge losses of social time, to the demands of commuting to a work that is more often a necessity for economic survival rather than a choice for personal development. Indeed, buried in the numbers of those who have been removed from the tax net is the fact that contemporary Ireland is operating on the basis of a low-wage economy with highly educated young people being paid wages far below the level of what is required to live.

We must, I suggest, conclude that our current, over-determined model of the economy, and the economic space, is reductionist, anti-social and limiting. We have a further example of this when we come to consider the issues associated with regional planning. Providing a level playing field for development, in any version of the economy, requires forms of infrastructure that cannot be left to emerge as casual results of the market economy. It simply has not happened anywhere where successful regional development has occurred. If regional balance is to be attained, it requires State initiative, be it in terms of ensuring connectivity for the region or providing vital forms of infrastructure.

A party of the Left has to be concerned about the absence of critical capacity that prevails at the present time, be it in the conventional political discourse, or, even more seriously, in a media that has lost the competence for context, not to speak of informed critical capacity.

In our contemporary lives in Ireland, we have entered into an era of unfreedom, of over-bureaucratisation – the very antithesis of a republican life. Max Weber, whose work in the fields of politics, religion, sociology and economics has been so enduring, described such a situation as a 'polar night of icy darkness', in which such an increasing rationalisation of human life emerges as traps individuals in an iron cage of rule-based, rational control – a rationalisation gone wrong, where what is predictable is a misery based on the loss of discretion or control over one's life, one's work, one's time, one's institutions. Indeed, when Weber himself was asked what his learning meant to him, he replied: 'I want to see how much I can endure.'

In a republic such as ours, such a version of life ought to give particular pause for thought. We fought hard in the past to bring our State into existence as an independent entity. That such a struggle might merely bring into existence a country where alienation – at times of economic growth – is widespread, and where the citizen is so wholly separated from the mechanism of the State, is shameful. It poses very basic questions as to what it actually means to be a citizen; what rights the individual can expect to have as part of society, as well as how one is to construct, maintain, or participate in a properly functioning society on the basis of solidarity.

It bears repeating that there needs to be a critical engagement – a critical relationship to, and a critical evaluation of, the society. There is a real need to engage critically with the world around us, particularly with regard to the way it is presented to us.

We are told again and again in Ireland, and by the OECD, at our own request, that our future demands that we be functional cogs within what is termed the 'knowledge economy'. This, it is suggested, is to make us 'competitive' – to ensure that we have a capacity, a facility, to compete with other zones of economic power. This may be true in the short term, but the risk it carries in terms of skills and capacity is that it is a recipe for obsolescence. What is needed is an economics based on creativity, a creative society making innovation possible, and making the living of a full life possible for all citizens.

Respecting the cultural space, then, is a value of the Left. Abusing or neglecting culture is a feature of the Right. Cultural policy, too, can prevent and treat some of the emerging tensions of our society: it can help us understand the many facets of sustainability. It can bring about a new sense of solidarity. It can positively inspire the new economy, and function as a means of empowerment and facilitate active citizenship. It can be the bedrock we need to reach out from to understand and respect other cultures with self-reliance.

In other words, it is an ingredient of society and policy which needs to be brought in from the margins, because for many decades it has not received the attention it deserves from policy-makers.

Sadly, today, across many parts of the world, culture is seen to be residual. It is marginal, tangential, and, in the worst instances, abandoned.

At the most practical level, despite spin and bluster, we still have no properly thought-out national spatial strategy, no regional policy, and no clear strategy for balanced and sustainable development. The west of Ireland, for example, lags significantly behind in investment, and even in the spending of European structural funds that were available for investment and regional development.

While we have managed to rid ourselves of the scourge of emigration, we have replaced it with an internal migration: during the last ten years of misguided government, vast numbers of our villages and towns are emptying while our cities are expanding exponentially. Such is the crush in the cities that people seeking to buy property can do so only in dormitory areas far from the city centres, in hastily built developments which require lengthy commutes into the city, in public transport for which there has been a hopelessly inadequate provision. We are thus creating unplanned urban diseconomies at the same time as we abandon social and physical infrastructure to decay.

It is such a combination of factors that demolishes our social fabric. It diminishes severely our social capital, as well as the quality of life of so many. It reduces growing swathes of the population to a treadmill existence, whereby they have little time to properly take part in life surrounding them, or to participate in, or help create, a sense of local community.

This is where alienation from the world at large takes hold, and it is one of the most pernicious elements of life in modern Ireland. It is a kind of betrayal of the very laudable and commendable ideals with which our forebears began the journey towards statehood, and the declaration of the Republic. Weber's view of the 'polar night of icy darkness' comes close to reality in this way.

If we were then to build a real republic, we must accept that building a real and inclusive citizenship is something that has to go far beyond making an appeal for volunteering. It requires the acceptance of the implications of a life beyond the self – the obligations, duties and rights that arise in the social. The reality of life foisted upon so many in Ireland is not only one of exclusion. It is also one of experiencing overbearing levels of bureaucracy, supposedly to aid, but more accurately to distance, the people from interaction with those public services that are supposed to represent and serve them. At a general level, quangos have come to proliferate, while parliamentary accountability has eroded to such a degree as to make parliament a charade. What is necessary, of course, is the extension and deepening of democracy, not its curtailment.

In the period between now and the local and European elections, members of the party must take the responsibility of carrying the campaign for the recovery of the public world, reconnecting the economy with society, and building inclusiveness. We have a clear agenda, and practical policies, that will rebuild trust, restore ethics to politics, and reform our public institutions.

We will spell out what we mean by universalism as the fundamental principle for the provision of public services. We will repeat our defence of collective representation and extend it. This will be part of our vindication of the dignity of work and the rights of workers, wherever they work, and from wherever they come.

We will do all this not because we have calculated some short-term advantage from policies that are so clearly better than those which prevail at present. We will do so because it is what a party of the Left should do. We will also be promoting these policies not just for our own generation but for future generations, because we believe that the new politics of the future is one that accepts inter-generational responsibility in relation to the society, including the economy, environment, heritage and planning.

The success of our political project will come primarily from our own commitment and our courage, above all else, in putting forward our values as a viable and decent alternative, one that deserves the support of the citizens of a real republic.

Presidential address to Labour Party Conference,
16 November 2007

5.

Responding to the Crisis

One of the most widely used terms to describe the present position of Irish society is that of 'crisis'. The word is being used not merely to describe the economic circumstances in which we find ourselves but also to refer to a deeper crisis of institutions in which the public has lost trust, be they in the realm of the state or civil society.

There is, however, a yet deeper feeling of crisis – one that goes beyond a crisis of expectations, perhaps veering through anger towards an inchoate nihilism: a destructive feeling of impotence capable of a great inter-generational despair and a loss of social cohesion, resulting perhaps in a violence that becomes widespread and vicarious. How should the Left, and Labour, respond to this?

The form which the crisis takes in economic terms is most dramatically illustrated by the rise in unemployment. The percentage of persons unemployed is 13.4 percent. In describing unemployment, however, it is very important to accept that every one of the 452,882 people that make up such a percentage are people whose lives have taken a huge impact of a negative kind, or whose hopes or expectations have been dashed.

Based on seasonally adjusted figures from the Department of Social Protection, the increase in numbers of those persons seeking employment in June is expected to be approximately 5,800. The overall unemployment figures do include more than 63,000 people who work part-time and more than 23,000 people who sign on to claim credits. Participation in the back-to-education allowance scheme has doubled this year, and more than 5,600 of the inflow in the first three weeks of June are from this scheme. Yet, for all these people the current time is one of anxiety – anxiety and worse for those not offered a choice.

The figure to be announced by the Central Statistics Office for June 2010 is, I repeat, 452,882. This is the highest number of people ever unemployed in the State. It is 300,000 more than were on the live register when the last general election took place in May 2007. It represents 100,000 jobs lost for each year that the government, in its present form, has been in office, and 2,000 jobs lost each week.

These figures of course do not include the number of people who have left the country, as immigrants who have gone home, or young Irish people who have emigrated to Australia and elsewhere.

As you heard last night from young people themselves, one in every three young men in the workforce is out of work. It is the cause of huge worry to parents who wonder whether their children will get work or whether history will repeat itself from their parents' time in the 1950s and they will have to emigrate. It is estimated that there may have been as many as 100,000 such emigrations since the beginning of the crisis, and the number is growing. The Central Statistics Office's recent figures suggest that 40 percent of those seeking work have been doing so for more than a year.

The impact of unemployment is far greater than the loss of income. It radically alters the form of participation of the unemployed person and their family in society. The level of poverty experienced by households impacts on not just the self-esteem and morale of the individuals out of work but also on their dependants and those who live with them. Their citizenship is radically changed. If we recall Amartya Sen's rough definition of equality of citizenship – 'the ability to participate in one's society without shame' – then for the unemployed, and those who depend on them, their lives, their citizenship, has radically changed.

In recent days, there has been talk of a return to growth, of the corner having been turned, yet the lessons of economic events and the commentary is that the economy, artificially defined, may recover and the people continue to suffer. A return to growth without addressing unemployment is to accept a de-peopled version of the economy.

The [Fianna Fáil-led] government's failure to prioritise the banking crisis in terms of solvency or liquidity, and its failure to address the needs of the real economy, is having the disastrous consequence of turning a recession into a depression. The failure to initiate a strategy for employment protection and creation is thus condemning individuals and families to poverty and exclusion, to a diminished form of citizenship.

History is being allowed to repeat itself as we offer a labour market subsidy, through emigration, to our competitors abroad. The government seems to have accepted the loss of 100,000 (mostly young) people to emigration. We have educated a young population regarded as among the most flexible workers in Europe, and the government is now exporting a huge proportion of this generation.

The government is also indicating that it may return to what is left in the National Pension Reserve Fund for further recapitalisation of the banks, including the two failed entities that have no future: Anglo Irish Bank and Irish Nationwide Building Society.

Labour has proposed a positive alternative, costed at about

€2 billion, for what is left in the National Pension Reserve Fund. We have suggested the establishment of a National Strategic Investment Bank, which would be a key building block in our jobs strategy. Already the cuts announced by government in the public finances, combined with the massive increase in savings, have had the effect of such a deflation in the economy as to send unemployment soaring.

The appeal to patriotism made by the government does not appear to have influenced the speculative decisions of those fleeing the euro for the dollar. In 2008, Irish-held US Treasury Bonds increased from €15 billion to €50 billion in a twelve-month period.

At a more local level, it is absolutely crazy for the government to remove €1 billion from its capital programme at a time when male unemployment in the construction industry is at an all-time historic high. At precisely the time when government could be providing infrastructure, schools, clinics, amenities and recreational facilities at the most competitive cost, when professionals such as architects, engineers and lawyers are unemployed or facing emigration, above all when so many construction workers are unemployed, the government cuts its capital spending.

This year, capital spending will comprise 5 percent of GNP; half of that which was allocated for 2010 is not spent; the equivalent figure for 2016 will be 3.1 percent. Meanwhile, social protection remains well below the European average. The inescapable result is an increase in unemployment and an escalation in the risk of poverty.

The government seems intent on sequencing its strategy in terms of starting with banking recapitalisation, then waiting for global growth, and simply hoping that, following an increase in exports, unemployment will begin to fall at that point. In the Finnish crisis, which was similar to Ireland's, even after a return to modest growth, unemployment did not fall significantly for a full five years.

Labour's Strategic Investment Bank could leverage a multiple of what it gets from the National Pension Reserve Fund so as to provide necessary infrastructure at the most competitive cost in decades. It is an employment-rich proposal. In addition, Labour's Strategic Investment Bank is the most practical way of getting high-grade employment in research and development.

A recent, excellent report from TASC highlighted, amongst other practical proposals, the fact that attached to third-level colleges and universities at the present time are about 350 incubated companies in the high-knowledge area, on which the government spends about €1 billion per year. Dr Tom O'Connor pointed out that thirteen companies were spun out of this as fully fledged trading companies; yet, all these companies, left without seed or development capital, were at the mercy of foreign multinationals that could purchase, at minimal cost, what had been created from research and development funded by Irish taxpayers.

If the Strategic Investment Bank that Labour has proposed had been in place, instead of a few dozen jobs, hundreds, even thousands, of first-rate, highly skilled jobs could have been created.

Using measures like the Strategic Investment Bank is a crucial approach to providing seed capital and liquidity. It is dishonest to suggest that the recapitalised banks will do so, or that we should wait for them. They have neither the record nor the intention of becoming primary agents in the real economy.

The work of TASC is replete with suggestions as to how a job-rich version of the social economy might be initiated. There are also, of course, jobs to be created in the green economy: the proposal Dr O'Connor has made for capitalising innovative discoveries from third-level sites is but one example. Job creation can also come from expanding the caring community and recognising the skills of carers and their valuable contribution – and indeed the savings that accrue to the State.

Again, in the cultural sector there are many opportunities for high-value, sustainable and personally rewarding job creation. A study by DKM economic consultants in 2009 reported that employment dependent on the creative and cultural sectors combined was 170,000 in 2008, or 8.7 percent of total employment. This sector is the fastest-growing sector in the global economy, representing 7 percent of global GDP, and growing at 10 percent per annum. Expenditure on this sector by the State represents a multiplier far greater than in many other areas.

DKM give figures for total Exchequer expenditure in 2008 of €330 million. The direct Exchequer revenue was approximately €1 billion, and the yield, taking the multiplier into effect, was €4.1 billion.

It is clear that a fundamental difference between Labour and the other parties is that we put employment creation, adequately capitalised, in a real economy, as a priority. If we are, however, to have what is no less than a paradigm shift in economic and political thinking, the community demand for it must come into existence, and a new form of economic literacy must emerge, one that challenges the present orthodoxy, which has failed.

Labour demands that the real economy now take priority, and we call for public support for our campaign for the unemployment crisis to be regarded as our present greatest challenge. Neither the unemployed, nor the real economy, can wait for the government to complete its mercy mission to a speculative banking system, before it engages with the real economy.

I also want to address what I believe is an aspect of the contemporary crisis that is not getting the attention it deserves – a crisis of language, of intellectual assumptions, of morality itself, and of the connection between economics and society.

Citizens are invited to accept as inevitable, as an inexorable law, a version of rationality in the markets that every aspect of their lives contradicts. They are bullied into accepting irrationality and chaos as the only version of reason and order.

Language itself becomes meaningless, becomes a threat rather than an instrument of liberation, when it is used to justify and sustain assertions that are not open to critical examination. It was Václav Havel who once said: 'Language can kill as easily as language can liberate.'

Literally every response to contemporary economic circumstances refers to 'the markets' and their response to the financial strategies of governments, those who speak for them, and the proposals of opposing spokespersons. The consequence of this is to lift a determining aspect of our lives out of the frame of accountability, transparency, or public understanding. The parallel with the medieval frame of reference is striking. Contemporary discourse rarely, if ever, seeks to provide a justification for the acceptance of what is a contestable 'domain assumption', a taken-for-granted fact, in the social sciences. There is nothing empirically inevitable about 'the market'; rather, it is an ideological assertion.

At our meeting last year, I suggested that there was an intellectual and academic background to our present crisis. The present economic crisis, with its misery of nearly thirty million unemployed people in Europe, the prospect of half a million unemployed people in Ireland, and half of the people on the planet living in abject poverty, is in its contemporary version based on a radical individualism.

From where did this intellectual departure come? In the modern period, it is worth recalling the injunction of Friedrich von Hayek, the high priest of radical market theory. His view was that the market order was beyond human comprehension, but necessary:

> The aim of the market order is to cope with the inevitable ignorance of everybody, of most of the particular facts which determine this order. By a process which men did not understand, their activities have produced an order much more extensive and comprehensive than anything that could comprehend it, but on the functions of which we have become utterly dependent.

There were, of course, a small number of economists who contested this myth of the rationality of markets. The Galbraiths, both father and son, at different periods, are among them. Others have been reluctant to let the myth go. Some seek an escape to the past. Amartya Sen, in a new preface to Adam Smith's *The Theory of Moral Sentiments*, clings to Smith's moral raft. He ignores, however, how reason was the concept that gave Adam Smith's economics its connection to morality.

Reason became rationality; that became calculable rationality; that in turn became market calculable rationality; and thus emerged the speculative vortex that has delivered global misery. How can Amartya Sen make his way back to reason? It is impossible without acknowledging the need for a paradigm shift.

While such a statement can be seen as having supplied, in the past, a manifesto for Thatcherism or Reaganism, it still remains as a source of policy in many areas of the world. Indeed, the views of von Hayek and Robert Nozick have, rightly, been described by Professor Michael Volkerling as constituting little less than a framework for 'a utopia of the Right', based on the separateness of persons. Von Hayek invoked a utopia of market extremism, and, while he had to wait decades, it emerged.

Von Hayek ushered in a new narrative in economics which has in recent times come to be accepted as something that cannot be questioned, as a form of inevitability. Professor Volkerling, in his paper, quotes a 1947 statement of Schumpeter which defined a new type of hero in this unaccountable economics. The characteristics of such a hero he described as one who was willing

> to act with that confidence beyond the range of familiar beacons, and to overcome that resistance requires aptitudes that are present in only a small fraction of the population, and [they] define the entrepreneurial type as well as the entrepreneurial function.

It is one of the distinctive aspects of the Labour Party's agenda that, rather than seeking to mend that which should not be mended, that to which we should not return, it both envisions, and offers as policy, a real alternative of an inclusive society based on a social economy in a world of responsible, fair, sustainable development.

In pursuing this alternative, the Labour Party is drawing on the rich legacy of socialist and emancipatory writing, including the utopian tradition.

The human impulse is to long for a better world. What Labour proposes must, then, address not just the basic needs of humans but must seek to develop the flowering of human potential achieved collectively. This rich tradition and scholarship, the emancipatory politics, this celebration of the power of the collective, has in recent times across Europe, particularly since 1989, been surrendered to an alternative. It was falsely assumed that a society could be achieved which would offer a sufficiency through consumer gratification within prevailing notions of the market. We are reaping the fruits of that false choice in many places in Europe and the world at the moment.

In 2009 I made the case for a return to the message of the liberating and empowering utopian literature. It is worth repeating just two quotations from Vincent Geoghegan's *Utopianism and Marxism*. In the first, Geoghegan makes the point, following Ernst Bloch, that hope must be grounded and must lead to a strategy for action and change. Reflection must result in action:

> For Bloch, the enemies of hope are confusion, anxiety, fear, renunciation, passivity, failure and nothingness. Fascism was their apotheosis. But since all individuals daydream, they also hope. It is necessary to strip this dreaming of self-delusion and escapism, to enrich and expand it and to base it in the actual movement of society. Hope, in other words, must be both educated and objectively grounded; an insight drawn from Marx's great discovery: 'the subjective and objective hope-contents of the world'.[1]

Geoghegan also finds in Bloch's *The Principle of Hope* an affirmation that preparing for future alternatives does not require any amnesia as to the past:

> *The Principle of Hope* is an encyclopaedic account of dreams of a better existence; from the most simple to the most complex; from idle daydreams to sophisticated images of perfection. It develops a positive sense of the category 'utopian', denuded of unworldliness and abstraction, as forward dreaming and anticipation. All the time, however, the link between past, present and future is stressed – concern with what one might be is the royal road to what one has been, and what one is:

---

1. E. Bloch, *The Principle of Hope*, Oxford: Basil Blackwell 1986, three volumes, 7.

'we need the most powerful telescope, that of polished utopian consciousness, in order to penetrate precisely the nearest nearness'.[2, 3]

For some this approach is tedious. Social democracy, even socialism, is too slow. Standing against any affirmation that real gains can be made, in terms of fighting for changes in social structures or forms of economy, is the radical writing of such as Slavoj Žižek:

> Today's 'mad dance' . . . awaits its resolution in a new form of Terror. The only 'realistic' prospect is to ground a new political universality by opting for the *impossible*, fully assuming the place of the exception, with no taboos, no a priori norms ('human rights', 'democracy'), respect for which would prevent us from 're-signifying' terror, the ruthless exercise of power, the spirit of sacrifice . . . if this radical choice is decried by some bleeding-heart liberals as *Linksfaschismus*, so be it![4]

This is a heady invitation to the unrestrained energy of youth in particular. It sneers at what it sees as long struggles, and thus makes non-sectarian Left co-operation difficult.

There are some on the Left who accept this view and suggest that the only authentic act of liberation from institutional terror must be, by definition, a confronting and undermining terror, a violent response. Many ethically minded people have been attracted to such a view and have paid a high price for their belief.

This is, I believe, a profoundly pessimistic view. While the changes that are urgent cannot be met by the fruits of Labour in the parliamentary process alone, the parliamentary process still

---

2. E. Bloch, *The Principle of Hope*, Oxford: Basil Blackwell 1986, three volumes, 12.
3. Vincent Geoghegan, Utopianism and Marxism, Bern: Peter Lang 2008, Chapter 'Ernst Bloch and the Ubiquity of Utopia', 115-16.
4. Butler, Laclau and Žižek, 2000, 326.

represents the best location and the best prospects for such a discourse as will enable the shape of a different society and a social economy to emerge.

That having been said, it is important that I enter a caveat to what I perceive to be the excessive optimism of such scholars as Jürgen Habermas in the possibilities of achieving a rational discourse, with a supporting consensus, that could enable the economy to become an instrument for the achievement of public welfare.

In this regard the work of Allyn Fives is relevant. He acknowledges that the generation of such a discourse has certain requirements, poses challenges, challenges that may not be easy to meet by some antagonists.

Habermas is admirable in his defence of the capacity for change in the public world, but again one might ask: what of the reason that has become an irrationality? One must question the silence, so general elsewhere, in academic philosophical writing on the disaster that has been delivered by assuming rationality in uncontrolled markets.

What began as reason in classical economic theory has become an irrational, speculative force, one that has created, and is creating, misery in different forms at a global level. It is this unaccountable irrationality that represents the most serious obstacle to such global challenges as climate change, the food crisis, global poverty and sustainable development.

There is at present another suggestion that has emerged from an extreme of communitarianism to the effect that one can retreat from the state and its parliamentary representative organs – as it were, start all over again with a *tabula rasa*. Its proponents include Charles Taylor and Alasdair MacIntyre, who, while they may differ in their degree of pessimism, clearly agree on withholding hope from existing parliamentary strategies or expressions.

I believe that these views, as I have previously said, could have disastrous consequences. However well meant, these views constitute a form of surrender of spaces within the state – spaces won at great cost. It is a surrender to the powerful forces of reaction.

If we have such large-scale unemployment, with such deeply excluding forms of inequality as its consequences, how is it, one may ask, that it is repeated so successfully, transmitted from one generation to another? How does this succeeding inequality reproduce itself? One of the factors that facilitates such a reproduction is embedded individualism and its dissemination, but also an uncritical scholarship, one which masks, or at best tendentiously describes, the existing status quo rather than uncovering the assumptions upon which it is built.

The challenge of inter-generational justice makes a new moral confrontation to such scholarship. Why should the uncritical actions of one generation become the irreversible burden of a succeeding one?

The task of demystification, of building such a new literacy to expose bogus expertise, is one that members of the Labour Party and beyond must embrace. We simply cannot afford to live as uncritical participants in an unequal society on a planet that moves ever further away from sustainability.

We need a new, engaged form of citizenship. This will not be easily attained, insofar as what has crept into the heart of some seemingly progressive policies of the Left in Europe in the last three decades is an acceptance of the very individualism which made it possible for the promise of the values associated with solidarity to be not so much rejected as lost.

There are tools that are available to us. We can connect with each other through the internet, exchange information – powerful tools. Yet we must remember the power achieved in the public space by marches, banners, songs, meetings, rhetoric, all of which, among other things, gave courage to the week and tentative, built solidarity with rights, and changed so much of the world. Of course, these need not be mutually exclusive.

We need a new politics of solidarity. We need an engaged, critical scholarship. We need a discourse which will envisage the alternative, inclusive society and the new social economics. This is what Ernst Bloch called 'anticipatory illumination'. It is not only about the right to survive. It is about the right to flourish.

In the short term it is necessary to stress again that standing as an alternative to the abstract entity of the markets is a form of society built on the principle of solidarity. This in the short term, and as an immediate baseline for Labour in government, means establishing a floor of citizenship below which no citizen would be allowed to fall.

Such a floor becomes the guarantee which is the precondition for any negotiation. Above-the-line matters may indeed be articulated, evaluated, and become a matter for negotiation as to priority. Only above this line can there be negotiation with those with whom one wishes to share a government. In a republic, the right to shelter, food security, education, a good environment, and freedom from fear and insecurity from childhood to old age, must be the benchmarks.

In the absence of a consideration which faces up to the task of examining the assumptions upon which our present economy and social structures are built, there are many false directions that the current debate is taking. As a substitute to the debate on deepening democracy, we have a debate on shrinking institutions; indeed, their abolition.

This extreme institutional reductionism, combined with slash-and-burn economics, is securing short-term support based on shallow analysis. It is hard not to conclude that such approaches are simply a response to populist pressure. The anger of disappointed expectations built on individualism after all is an anger which can be easily misdirected.

It is a real task – for many it may be impossible – to get back to, or arrive at, the principle that security, development and prosperity have to be achieved collectively. The Irish people have had no adequate debate on what the citizenship required for this means or demands; rather, what they have had is a discussion on volunteering from portions of private time, and philanthropy from portions of private income, as substitutes for public provision, all of which accept the basic premise of individualism and none of which accepted in full the demands of community and solidarity.

Should the adjustment in economic and social assumptions prove to be incapable of being made, we probably face an unmediated confrontation between the excluded and those who chose to be unconcerned. Such a point is the one at which the dark prescriptions of Slavoj Žižek become relevant. Around the world there is evidence that such an outcome is achieving momentum, and some support.

If parliamentarianism is to work, it will require deep and radical institutional change. That change, however, must be one that achieves the opportunity of making parliament relevant to the great issues of the day. It is not about numbers or the detail of practice; it is rather about creating new opportunities for relevance and participation.

Irish politics is in need of reform; on that there is general agreement. In response to the loss of trust visited on the public by individuals and institutions political and financial, an adequate response is both urgent and unavoidable. There is, however, a real danger that by concentrating on the wrong part of the task of reform, the entire effort may end up as simply the feeding of a dangerous populism rather than achieving the changes that are necessary.

I believe we should not shrink from a fundamental examination and reform of the legislative process itself. To achieve this, it is important not to begin in the wrong place. A concentration on reform of the electoral process without, for example, examining the role and function of those who are elected to parliament and from whose numbers government will be formed by whatever electoral system, the exclusive powers given to those appointed to Cabinet or those holding senior positions in the public service, the transparency and accountability in terms of their legislative effectiveness and capacity afforded, would be a futile exercise.

Recent decades have seen the Dáil lose accountability to a plethora of extra-parliamentary bodies. As a consequence there has been a serious erosion of transparency and accountability. For example, a Parliamentary Question to the Minister for Transport on a matter on roads or traffic impact in one's constituency may well not be answered in the Dáil on the basis that authority in this matter has been ceded to the National Roads Authority. Similarly, a question to the Minister for Health and Children on a health matter, which is deemed to have been delegated to the Health Services Executive, will be disallowed.

These are but some of the more serious and recent examples of leaks from parliamentary accountability. While the agencies specified may indeed have a parliamentary section to answer parliamentary enquiries, the erosion of accountability is obvious. A constitutional issue, indeed, arises as to what precisely the Minister involved in such a delegation must specify, what the boundaries of what is policy and what is an administrative matter are. In this area, there is no clarity, and a serious question arises as a consequence as to whether the responsibility of the Minister to parliament, as understood in the constitution, has been eroded.

Any serious examination of the process of making, changing, and implementing legislation in Ireland would thus have to acknowledge a serious case for reform of a general and fundamental kind. Unfortunately, proposals for reform in recent times, drawn from a recently recovered interest, have been aimed, almost exclusively, at simply where the populist dividend is highest – changing the voting system – thus making the prospects for real reform far less promising.

Perhaps it is that so many aspects of Irish society, consumed in their consumption in an artificial version of the economy, no longer possess the capacity to articulate any alternative, any way out of our contemporary crisis. At first glance, it appears that much has not changed. The suggestion that banks get back to the way that they were, that an old version of authority must be restored within institutions, including even the Church, that austerity must be imposed, that services must be cut, has still quite a wide acceptability among the public. Is it the case that either of the largest parties in the State favours a new departure in any aspect of our society? I am afraid the signs are negative.

That is why a great responsibility falls upon the Labour Party to be the real alternative. This will require a great effort from the membership. It will be necessary to be able to take charge of a discourse on the economy, on social inclusion, on climate change. We cannot afford to assume that others will do the work that will bring us to where we want to be. After all, as I have demonstrated, there are other, powerful interests who not only do not share our values, but are completely opposed to them.

In the coming decade, the role of the State will be defined anew. We need a state system that is genuinely inclusive, and that is participatory. There is much to be changed, including all the forms of negative bureaucracy that have extended and atrophied the system.

In our contemporary lives in Ireland we have been for some time in an era of unfreedom, of over-bureaucratisation – the very antithesis of a republican life. Max Weber, whose work in the fields of politics, religion, sociology and economics has been so enduring, described such a situation as a 'polar night of icy darkness', in which such an increasing rationalisation of human life emerges as traps individuals in an iron cage of rule-based, rational control – a rationalisation gone wrong, where what is predictable is a misery based on the loss of discretion or control over one's life, one's work, one's time, one's institutions.

In a republic such as ours, such a version of life ought to give particular pause for thought. We fought hard in the past to bring our State into existence as an independent entity. That such a struggle might merely bring into existence a country where alienation – at times of economic growth – is widespread, and where the citizen is so wholly separated from the mechanism of the State, is shameful. It poses very basic questions as to what it actually means to be a citizen; what rights the individual can expect to have as part of society; as well as how one is to construct, maintain, or participate in a properly functioning society on the basis of solidarity.

It bears repeating that there needs to be a critical engagement; a critical relationship to, and a critical evaluation of, the society. There is a real need to engage critically with the world around us, particularly with regard to the way it is presented to us.

In two years' time, the Labour Party will be celebrating the hundredth anniversary of our founding by brave people who had courage, conviction, and the principle to stand against the tide in favour of a real republic. Now that Labour is surging ahead in the polls, we have not only an opportunity to emulate their efforts, redefine our values in new conditions, and, most important of all, invite all members of the public to be with us in building a real alternative with Labour.

Address to Tom Johnson Summer School,
Kilkenny, 3 July 2010

6.

The Democratic Programme
of the First Dáil

For Labour, Vision of a Possibility;
For Others, an Exercise in Bad Faith

When the twenty-four Sinn Féin candidates out of the sixty-nine who had been elected met as the first Dáil on 21 January 1919, the Democratic Programme of the First Dáil was the most important document that was, with full solemnity, placed before them. It was placed before them, however, in circumstances that might correctly be regarded as unwelcoming. The Irish Republican Brotherhood had not approved of the document and indeed Michael Collins had undertaken to suppress it.

Piaras Béaslaí, who moved it at the meeting, would speak later of the little support there would have been for it had it come to a vote because, as he put it, 'many objected to the communistic flavour of the document':

> It is doubtful whether the majority of the members would have voted for it without amendment had there been any immediate prospect of putting it into force . . .
> If any charge of insincerity could be made against this first Dáil, it would be on this score. (Mitchell p. 109)

Kevin O'Higgins would later refer to it as 'largely poetry'. Arthur Griffith, who with others was in jail and therefore precluded from attending the historic meeting, was not only opposed to its assumptions and principles but had written comprehensively in that regard before the meeting.

Nevertheless, the document, even after the editing of Seán T. Ó Ceallaigh, is the substantial document of the meeting of the First Dáil on 21 January 1919. Drafted as it was by Tom Johnson, assisted by William O'Brien and Cathal O'Shannon, it is a powerful statement of what was possible for the democratic state that might have been created. In his *Labour and Irish Politics 1890-1930*, Arthur Mitchell describes how Cathal O'Shannon and Tom Johnson watched the moving of the document from the gallery, with O'Shannon anxious at the deep emotion displayed by his fellow author.

The document had been amended by Ó Ceallaigh in order not just to tone down what the Labour leaders had drafted, but also to take account of the earlier revision of Pearse's notion of sovereignty and the public ownership of Ireland's natural resources. The Ó Ceallaigh papers obliquely claim authorship for the Democratic Programme for Ó Ceallaigh himself.

Why was the document moved? It seems clear to me that the opportunity to secure recognition for the new Irish state was the reason for the declaration that was to be called the Democratic Programme of the First Dáil being moved. This opportunity for recognition was, indeed, later availed of by Tom Johnson and Cathal O'Shannon while they were attending the first post-war conference of the Socialist International in Berne. Eamon de Valera was later to say 'when we wanted the help of Labour in Berne, Labour gave it to us and got Ireland recognised as a distinct nation'.

For those Labour leaders who watched in the gallery, the moving of the Democratic Programme of the First Dáil was a dream articulated and made attainable. It was the shining evidence of a possibility being expressed at the birth of a state, a vision that was powerfully egalitarian, celebratory, asserting a deep humanity, and linked to an international movement that was pushing a great change towards a socialist version of politics, economy and society. The Labour authors were not merely utopian. They were, as internationalists, part of a process of democratic change.

The Democratic Programme gave a glimpse of the possibility of dealing with the injustices that motivated the founders of Labour – that is, of eliminating poverty, inequality, the exploitation of vulnerable workers; of advancing the rights of women and children; of dealing with inadequate access to education and health care, amongst other things. The tragedy is that these themes have remained pertinent and in need of correction all through the history of the state, albeit not as brutally as when Labour was founded.

To those present, who were not asked to vote or comment on the document but who heard it read in Irish and English, it may have had different meanings. No doubt it was simply poetry to some, but to the more cynical it surely represented an exercise in bad faith. Certainly, all the policies and actions that followed, that flowed from the inheritance of a conservative Sinn Féin and its offshoots, ran counter to the principles expressed, be it in terms of the rights of children, women and property, or indeed of the state itself, to participate in the economy or give guarantees regarding social security. A deep conservatism and narrow-minded view of a fledgling state swiftly manifested itself by establishing property rights as superior to the rights, held in common, of citizens.

We should never forget Tom Johnson's reservations, expressed three years later, on behalf of the Labour Party, when the draft 1922 Constitution was circulated on the eve of an election in that year. He emphasised what it was that Labour had sought in the Democratic Programme and what the newly empowered native conservatives were proposing as an alternative.

The constitution which was proposed, he said, ran 'counter to our own Labour Party constitution, which sets out as one of our objects, "the abolition of all powers and privileges, social and political, of institutions or persons based upon property or ancestry or not granted or confirmed by the freely expressed will of the people". The genuine republicanism of this stands in marked contrast to the property-based conservatism of those who had now moved into positions of power in the state in its institutions – including, particularly, its universities.

From the first stirrings of an Irish labour movement, which sprang from an era of extreme difficulties and harshness in 1912-13, a vision emerged that could answer the immediate problems of working people but that also demanded the changes that were necessary in the structures of the economy, society and the political system. The Irish state, utterly dominated as it was by those in public office who looked inward, and who betrayed a lack of ambition, or worse, interest, in bettering the lives of so many working people, certainly did not succeed in the following years in achieving the goals as set out by Tom Johnson on behalf of Labour.

Labour, then, was consistent. Three years after the momentous reading to the Democratic Programme of the First Dáil, Labour had enshrined its principles in its first constitution. The parties with which it would eventually contest elections in the 1920s were already preparing for a conservative programme that would reach horrific proportions in the 1930s in terms of bigotry, censorship, social repression and a cowardly subjugation of the state and its institutions to unaccountable, hierarchical, patriarchal and undemocratic institutions in the economic, social, cultural and religious life of the nation.

It is not the case, therefore, of there ever having been a consensual acceptance of the Democratic Programme of the First Dáil that was later betrayed. The truth is that it was never accepted by many of those who heard it.

The Dublin Trades Council in March 1918 had first used the term 'Democratic Programme'. They understood what it meant and what it aspired to. Labour, even with all its divisions of the period, understood. Those who had suffered under the great Lockout knew what it might achieve. Sean O'Casey, whose plays illustrated the deprivation, but also the nobility, of the vast underclass in Dublin city, was well aware of the implications of the suggestion that social and economic equality must wait until England had left Ireland. He saw the native predators in the wings of the new state, just as Michael Davitt had seen the graziers coming after the Land War. Ireland could be free, tenants could get the land, and workers might still be enslaved, and the Dublin slums would remain as sites for bogus heroics.

Labour can be proud of the inspirational manifesto which it provided for that meeting of the First Dáil. The Dáil got on with the business of electing a Ceann Comhairle, clerks, deciding on its business, the reading of a Constitution, a Declaration of Independence, and a Message to the Free Nations of the World in Irish, English and French.

However, the document that might have spoken to the Irish people in the slums of the cities, to the remnants of the agricultural labourers, to the smallholders and the shop boys and girls who bore the brunt of the War of Independence, and who would later divide in a Civil War, was the Democratic Programme of the First Dáil.

They, who had taken the greater risks in both wars, were not in the Mansion House.

The parallels between the conditions then and now are significant. There is the task of recrafting the connection between society and an economy collapsing owing to greed, stupidity and government connivance with speculative forces, on a basis of egalitarian values.

Labour's commitment remains to greater equality in the conditions of people's lives. It is a commitment to greater economic equality, to deepening democracy, both in the political system and in other areas of society, to universal education, to creativity, and to decent working conditions for all.

All these are commitments made in the Democratic Programme. The tragedy is that so many conservative governments over the years since the initial text was written have ensured that many of its aims remain aspirational. Whether derided as poetry, or abused as rhetoric, it remains a valuable, real and challenging document. It rightly and appropriately constitutes the minimum demand for Labour's participation in any government.

18 January 2009

I would like to thank my colleague Brendan Halligan, with whom I shared so much both before and after his period as general secretary of the Labour Party, for his lecture on the Democratic Programme of the First Dáil. I would also like to express the indebtedness of the party to those distinguished scholars of Labour and the Left who have contributed to the Labour History Society and its journals. We are also indebted, of course, to those outside that group who have provided us with valuable essays and insights based on careful analysis of the papers that were made available from some of the main personages in the history of the early days of the twentieth century.

7.

Building a New Citizenship

Achieving the Real Alternative in Solidarity

This conference [in March 2009] takes place at a time of crisis in economic terms but also at a time when there is evidence of great anxiety and a desire and willingness to change.

We in Labour must respond with a critique that is as fearless as it is honest. We must be resolute and courageous too in setting out the basic elements of the new economy that needs to be built, the new connections between economy and society that are needed, the transparent reforms in governance that are demanded, and the role of the state in a mixed economy in recession.

When I say that we need to be fearless, by this I mean that we have to claim the space for a new and different discourse as well as giving that disclosure a content that is practical as well as inspirational.

The present economic morass in which we find ourselves cannot be regarded as the consequences of an accident. Its international dimension was sourced in a version of economics that was carefully propagated, and was based on a radical individualism on unregulated markets and an extension of financial instruments so as to include virtual products based on speculative estimates of growth and indebtedness.

The neo-liberal model of this economy drove all this growth without substance in production and export terms. Among the high priests of this madness was European Commissioner Charlie McCreevy. Having facilitated speculative alternatives to real growth at home, he later took to lecturing those in Europe who believed in the social economy that they were backward in not adopting the heady mix of liberalisation, privatisation and speculation in virtual financial instruments, all facilitated by regulation with a light touch.

For us now to address the way forward in economic terms, in such a way as will build social cohesion, we must be clear on what it is that constitutes the project of the Left as the only real alternative to that which has failed, with such disastrous social consequences.

Our project is not simply the demonstration of political incompetence. That speaks for itself. Neither can it be a resuscitation of that which has collapsed, with such disastrous consequences for citizens, including the prospect of more than 400,000 people being out of work. We have to state that the neo-liberal model of the economy and society has failed and that a new social model of the economy must be, and can be, put in its place.

Such a model is not simply more democratic, inclusive, sustainable, egalitarian and positive. It is also based on better economics.

The advocates of that which has failed have not gone away. Having prescribed a toxic medicine, they now seek a role as undertakers in the media. Refusing to recognise their failed model, they obscure the consequences of their wild irrational economic assumptions, their lethal policy prescriptions. Their response now would be as callously indifferent to the social implications of what they propose, by way of adjustment or response, as it was when they were advocating a radical individualism and supporting a trickle-down economics that required the existence of poverty as an incentive.

Dr Padraic Kenna, in his most recent book, quotes a report prepared for Investec Private Bank by DKM Consultants in 2008. It pointed out that €41 billion was added to the collective wealth of the richest 450 people in Ireland in the three years from 2005 to 2008. It spoke of 'quiet wealth' of around €11 billion accrued by those who sold land for property and such infrastructure as roads.

Dr Kenna states that housing is now the central repository of personal wealth, with a nominal value which rose from €39.1 billion in 1981 to €553.5 billion in 2005.

He also quotes a Bank of Ireland report in 2007, 'Wealth of the Nation', which showed that the asset base (defined as gross assets minus residential property) of the top 1 percent of the population increased from €86 billion in 2005 to €100 billion in 2006.

This is regarded by some as 'the good times'. Good for whom, one might well ask. Of course, most of this artificial growth would not have been possible had the Kenny Report, with its proposals to control the cost of building and essential land – a report which Labour consistently supported – been introduced.

While speculative fortunes were being enhanced in one Fianna Fáil/PD budget after another, Ireland remained among the worst countries for wealth distribution, as adjudged by the OECD. In 2006, it was in twenty-seventh place out of thirty countries. In the same year, while claiming to be the second-richest country in the European Union, and occasionally the world, Ireland had the second-lowest level of social protection. Social protection includes childcare, housing and amenity facilities, transport, and the basics in general for a decent housing and work environment.

We must remember that this version of the economy was possible because the parties who promoted it had political support. Maybe we should also remember R. H. Tawney's old observation on why there was public support for inequality. He gave the example of tadpoles who put up with their miserable conditions in the prospect that one of their number might sprout a jaw and leap to land and become a frog.

Perhaps it was so. We should remember too, however, that there was uncritical institutional support for this version of the economy from banks, higher echelons of the state, university presidents and county managers. There was general enthusiasm from what can be called the 'toxic elite' who hopped from one board to another, with different levels of financial agility and illegality. This toxic elite, we should remember, largely remains in place. It is these same people who now turn to the state and the taxpayer for succour and support, for guaranteed solvency for all their operations, including the toxic assets that were the source of their remuneration and bonuses. Keeping that show on the road has been, as many small businesses will be aware, at the cost of liquidity – a liquidity that is vital not just to create but also to retain jobs.

Already, of course, taxpayers are paying for the actions of that small toxic network. We are all doing so, insofar as the government borrows for day-to-day running of the country at a rate several points higher than the European average, on foot of the damage done to the country's reputation. A reputational capital built up over decades was squandered by the irresponsible actions of some of those who headed Anglo Irish Bank, those who chose not to inform themselves, those who were in charge of the public finances, responsible for governance and due diligence.

Let me make some suggestions. We cannot solve our immediate fiscal problems by addressing our demands solely to income. We have to recognise, and claw back a real contribution from, such wealth as has accrued to the speculative sources at the heart of the crisis.

CORI, in its socio-economic review of 2008, quotes a Goodbody's Economic Consultants report that shows that between 1999 and 2006, the urban renewal scheme, in terms of tax revenue forgone, was €1,423 billion for the seven years.

As far back as 2004, the Revenue Commissioners figures indicated that property tax reliefs had an annual cost of €8.4 billion each year. As CORI points out, this would amount to a figure equivalent to 22 percent of total taxation.

Not everybody benefited from what is called the boom of the Celtic Tiger years. Over 80 percent of those who benefited from tax relief from multi-storey car parks had incomes of over €200,000 in 2006. The more income you had to spare, the more you could use your accountant to benefit from the property tax relief.

Revenue Commissioners figures show that between 1999 and 2003 – four years – the number of top earners benefiting from very low tax levels, of less than 15 percent, had increased from 18.25 percent to 20 percent.

Indeed, of the top four hundred earners, three reduced their liability to zero, and forty-eight kept their liability below 5 percent.

From this, you can see why such people would need a bank of their own with a light-regulation touch.

Why is it, you might well ask, that it is so difficult for wealth to be discussed in contemporary Ireland? Many of the commentators who write endlessly of public expenditure and income tax find it very difficult to allow wealth to be mentioned. This is not accidental. There is more than an absence of time or scholarship involved. There is an exercise of caution in conditions where there is a strong tendency to monopoly in the media. It is a constant finding from wealth tax studies that opposition is based much more on what would be revealed by any wealth tax than on the issue of what the yield of such taxes might be.

The politicians of the Right who gave property-related tax breaks to those who thought paying tax was for little people, the politicians of the Right who sneered at the social provision of the Scandinavian social economies as backward and encouraging disincentives to individual wealth, gave us, as their alternative, regulation with a light touch. Thus they facilitated the degradation of governance and sacrificed trust at home and Ireland's reputation abroad. We should remember that they have not gone away, nor have they reformed. They were opposed by Labour at every step of the way, and will be until the consequences of their failed model is recognised and we have made a beginning on building its alternative: a responsible social model of the economy.

The politics of the Right cannot be the alternative that addresses our current situation or our prospects for the future. That politics is toxic in social economic terms and is recognised as such in one disaster area after another of the global economy. Economists such as Nobel Laureates Joseph Stiglitz and Amartya Sen have written of it in such terms.

Yet here in Ireland, where nobody on the Right admits a mistake, the old politics, the bad economics, is presented as the source of the alternative in a media often devoted more to celebratory comment than to any substantial critique. There is also what I am afraid I must call a certain moral cowardice involved among those who refuse to recognise the difference between the politics and the economics of the Right and the politics and economics of the Left. It is lazy to refer to all of them in the phrase 'the politicians', and thus tacitly to subscribe to the fiction that there is no difference between them. It is more than lazy, it is a serious contribution to public cynicism at best, and at worst a celebration of political ignorance.

Let it be said: Labour's policies did not deliver our present chaos. Labour's policies would have made a difference if they had been implemented. Labour's policies are the real alternative, based on equitable, ethical, transparent and achievable polices.

What is needed now is a campaign to build a new citizenship. That is the only true basis of a real solidarity. It is the best prospect for a return to trust – a trust that has been squandered at so many levels.

We need a viable political system, with clear options and real choices. We need a discourse that is capable of handling all the connections between economy, society and the State. This cannot be simply a discourse for experts; it must be a publicly informed discourse with real participation. Neither can we afford to jettison real and important areas of scholarship and policy such as economics, sociology, law and administration. We cannot afford to substitute a celebratory populism for real policy discussion, choice and decision. It is not a time for anti-intellectualism. Neither can the new citizenship we need to create be reduced to an appeal for voluntary activity. Much more than that is at stake.

In achieving this, and preparing in the short term, we should define a floor of rights and raise it progressively, and use our taxes to sustain it. A social economy can deliver a system of guarantees in relation to citizenship in terms of both security and participation. In the guarantees we give to break inter-generational poverty, to create true access and participation, we should not abandon our global pledge, already broken before, to the poorest of the poor. We must keep our revised commitment to the UN target for overseas development aid – reaching 0.7 of GNP in 2012.

We will need to redefine work, recognising its human character, going beyond its narrow utilitarian designation as solely paying for time spent in the traded economy. We must recognise the work of carers, for example, and call it employment in the social economy – which is what it is.

New combinations of health expenditure, social welfare and education support can be made to sustain activity in a rewarding sense, with both short- and long-term benefits to the person and the community, giving a more sustainable and creative life to parents and children.

Rather than having a slash-and-burn approach to the economy, we should come out of the recession with social protection enhanced, with real achievements in upskilling, and with creativity respected as the basis of innovation as we build the social economy. We must sustain jobs, protect jobs, create jobs in the social economy, in the green economy, in new technologies. We should purchase patents and technologies from abroad if necessary in the short term to make the best connection between a highly educated population and the international economy.

I repeat, we must recognise the employment potential that flows from the creativity, the creativity that is there in the cultural area. It will be the case in the future that economic models will be generated in a cultural space that is creative, rather than of culture activity being seen as residual to the economy.

There is growing support among the public for proposals that are both progressive and practical. There is nothing more practical than a sound economy where wealth is defined in terms of the welfare of all the people. Labour's policies appeal to the best instincts of the public.

What we have had — and that which has failed the many for the benefit of the few — was not inevitable. It was made possible by the politics of the Right. There is no single way. There is no single version of finance. There are choices all over the global economy.

For real policies, the questions cannot be avoided: is it your policy to repair that which is failed and failing, or to build something new on decent values, good engaged scholarship, transparent government? It must not be about keeping or repairing the rackets. It can be about being something truly different, achieving what we have the capacity to be – a real republic with citizenship values that are public and inclusive.

There is no point in a bogus consensus. Let those who hold such values as according a minimal role to the state in the economy, and who would limit the state as guarantor of social security, combine if they wish with those who share such values.

Labour will co-operate, will give a lead, with those who recognise, who commit, and are willing to participate, in the achievement of its genuine programme of building the social economy here, in Europe and beyond.

May I invite those who share so many of our values to join with us in a real social partnership. That is what is required when citizens are suffering from the policies and the neglect of the policies of the Right. The Left alternative is a shared vision. There are many outside Labour who hold values that are similar. All I ask is that they recognise that, and that in their appeals for reform and in their campaigns they draw the distinction between those who support them, those who oppose them, and those who are available for conversion. It is easy to fudge the issue with an appeal to the 'politicians' in some kind of assumed neutrality.

Such evasion can produce at best only a cynicism that is corrosive. I invite them to be with us and for us to work together, to recognise, at the very least, that we have chosen a similar road.

We are in new times. In a few years it will be a real achievement if we can accomplish what was envisaged ninety years ago in the Democratic Programme of the First Dáil, written by Tom Johnson, leader of the Labour Party. What better memory to have than to be able to say that we have worked together to create the foundations of a real republic, based on the needs, aspirations, imagination and genius of all our people in their different ways.

Support our candidates; elect our candidates. Invite others to be part of building the real alterative: Labour's alternative, the Left alternative. In the future, let us be proud to remember how, together, we built something new, both visionary and practical, as we said; that we were proud to be Left, proud to be Labour.

Address to the Labour Party Conference,
Mullingar, 27 March 2009

8.

The Present Economic and Political Crisis: Labour's Response

The fifth of June 2009 will be seen historically as an extremely significant day in the history of the Labour Party, and potentially, if the hard work is continued, as a turning point in Irish political history. To have elected three MEPs, 132 city and county councillors and 84 town councillors is no mean feat, and it is an achievement which reflects very well on the Labour Party as a whole. To have approximately 250 people elected to office across the country is a testament to talent, hard work and strong organisation, and it strengthens our hand in seeking to effect lasting change in Ireland.

To achieve that necessary and lasting change, we have to be very clear as to what we regard as the minimum we will seek to do if elected to government, and indeed what our minimum demands would be if elected in such numbers as would justify our participation in government. It is incumbent on us all to frame and state explicitly that which we regard as a baseline for our participation in government: what those things would be upon which we would insist, and enact, upon taking seats in government and in Cabinet.

While those of us here may all share much of the same general view on this – that we will insist on a society where participation is based on citizenship and rights, rather than on the wealth that one possesses – we must realise that such a view may require to be imposed on those who will have to be forced to accept it as the price of office.

On the matter of the greatest crisis facing Ireland and the world at the present time, a global economic slowdown which serves as context for our own government's home-grown speculative property bubble in Ireland, it is vital that we present coherently and cogently our alternative economic view, and make the case for it strongly. We must work to achieve no less than a shift in consciousness; we have to achieve a demystification of the economic sphere. We must all be able to speak with confidence of our alternative economic strategy and to seek support for it with confidence and commitment.

The present economic crisis in which we are immersed has, as perhaps its worst feature, a catastrophic rise in unemployment. The level of unemployment is set to pass half a million. How we respond to this will reveal the differing political assumptions, the ideology, and the policies of the Left and the Right in Irish politics.

The basic thrust of the politics of the Right, in economic terms, is to give first priority to stabilising the banking system, even at the cost of a taxation impact on future generations. This is to be followed by a fiscal strategy that offers stability, even at the cost of cuts in vital public infrastructure, and cuts in wages that may be regressive in terms of net income and spending capacity.

Taken even on the basis of its own assumptions, this approach promises disaster. This sequencing of bank stability followed by a slash-and-burn fiscal strategy, which is demanded ahead of, or indeed as an alternative to, such a stimulus as would reflate the economy, will swiftly drive unemployment through the half-million barrier. Furthermore, whatever short-term yield comes from emergency taxation and cuts in capital programmes will be quickly absorbed by the cost of servicing the increases in unemployment in the form of social welfare payments. The shrinking of the economy through reductions in income and cuts in expenditure is a recipe for disaster.

It is possible, as a real alternative, to expand the economy with an investment strategy which would fill the gap in vital infrastructure, sustain and create employment in such areas as the construction industry, and create such demand as will sustain a retail sector that is under immediate and massive threat.

It is possible, furthermore, to do this with such careful auditing of its employment effect as to achieve the best possible effect within the boundaries of the economy. The suggestion that a stimulus package automatically leads to leaks from the economy is simply nonsense.

Again, the possibilities in the creative economy can be realised by investment in the economy rather than measures that cause it to contract. The multiplier effect from such economic activity is greater, more sustainable, and has a better regional distribution. Shrinking the economy so as to get back to a previous moment of preparation for speculation is simply to repeat the disaster from which we are seeking to escape.

As far as the Left is concerned, there really is no choice. We should stimulate the economy. I believe we should do so, in order to achieve a new form of social economy that is aimed in turn at achieving a real citizenship – with a floor below which citizens will not be allowed to fall in terms of social security and dignity at all ages, with a commitment to universal provision for the full participation in society without shame, as Amartya Sen puts it. Around such a project it is possible to build a real solidarity and an empowering consensus.

To do this, we need to drain the bogus inevitabilities of the

Right of their influence. The Right suggest that we accept an unemployment rate of one in six as somehow inevitable. The Right will shortly seek to reduce increased costs of unemployment by cutting social welfare expenditure, presenting its argument as a necessary step to enhanced competitiveness, as inevitable.

A further unstated assumption of the Right, of course, is the acceptance of the return of emigration as a safety valve for a society facing the crisis of an artificially bloated economy.

The support that economic commentators, as distinct from economists with a commitment to political economy in any scholarly sense, offer to such a superficial approach is more than disappointing; it is dangerous. Put simply, the narrow, simplistic models of cyclical theorists advising on the economy as an entity separate from its citizens are aimed at creating an abstract version of the economy – the economy as a de-peopled system, one that can ignore the human context in the short or medium term.

The Left, on the other hand, begins in the short term with the importance of sustaining income through job protection and job creation, arguing that this will in time create an economy that has recovered exports and returned to growth, even sustainable growth. That growth will be measured differently, however, to previous speculative growth, which was artificial, and had no genuine economic or social yield. It will be measured in terms of its contribution to social security, to the necessary infrastructure in physical, social and cultural terms of not only the present generation, but of future generations. In doing this, it will contribute positively to inter-generational justice rather than robbing future generations of their prospects.

The timescales, too, within which the economic policies of the Left and the Right function are fundamentally different – as different as the very purpose to which they are directed. The economics of the Right are based on the short-term consumption, without regard for distribution or equity, of disaggregated individuals, in the shortest possible term. The Left carries both the obligation and the prospects of a solidarity based on inclusion, creativity and participation in economic, social, temporal and spatial terms.

The intellectual and policy contradiction, and collision, between Right and Left on such grounds, then, cannot be avoided as we seek to address the full nature of the crisis in which we now find ourselves. It is more than an economic and social crisis; it is an intellectual and moral crisis – one that could get worse, even deliver disaster, as history tells us that such circumstances as now prevail could produce a response that leads to a right-wing authoritarianism as easily as to the making of a new beginning, or a revision of the assumptions that have brought us to this point.

The contemporary response to our present crisis reflects the gaps that have been created between morality, ethics, and economic and social policy. The de-peopled economy was the creation of such a split between the values of each of these branches of human reflection and existence. We have to recover from this and regain ground lost at the level of public discourse. Our scholarship has to be made whole again if it is to make a genuine contribution in human terms.

At times of crisis, too, there is always the danger of an early response offering the temptation to avoid the sources of the crisis. Rarely is there a speedy acknowledgment of error. In responding to the present crisis, we are very far from a sufficient acknowledgement of what it is that has created this crisis – of the political hegemony that delivered it, the scholarship that supported it, the fictions which created it, the media which celebrated the excess at its centre, or indeed the misguided citizens who gave their political assent to its assumptions, in the vain hope, no doubt, that they or their children might one day come to consume at the same level as the fantasists and celebrities whom they had admired as the icons and role models of their life.

Those who, in recent decades, were privileged to have the space for academic reflection but who offered compliance or silence, carry a great responsibility. A certainty was claimed by many scholars in the social sciences for prescriptions that were simply accommodations to the prevailing greed. Nowhere was this clearer than in the discussion on economic growth, on the rush to the acceptance of market extremism, the acceptance of deregulation, and the uncritical acceptance of the tenets of individualism as the alternative to a social consideration that was perceived as passé.

It is certainly worthy of our consideration too as to how so many aspects of our lives came, in recent decades, to be regarded as outside the capacity to understand of ordinary citizens, or in particular of their elected representatives. Does one lose one's capacity to analyse, understand or prescribe because one is elected? In recent times, it has been assumed as a given, in most sections of the media, that the public can never come to understand economics and that it is an area for such expertise as is possessed by only a few. In this claim for hegemonic expertise, we encounter something like the monopoly claimed, in previous times, in matters spiritual, by those dogmatists who suggested that fear and blind obedience were the necessary ingredients for a safe soul.

As to the profession of economics itself: John Maynard Keynes once wrote 'if economists could manage to get themselves thought of as humble, competent people on a level with the dentist, that would be splendid'. His advice is not being taken by those in the profession who are responding to the crisis, nor is it likely to be.

Nevertheless, while it is wise to reflect on what he suggested, we cannot afford to indulge in an anti-intellectualism which would regard it as acceptable to condemn the discipline of economics itself, or all the members of that profession. It is important, however, to recognise that standing behind the human chaos and tragedy, the unemployment, poverty and alienation, which are the features of our economic collapse, is a scholarship that facilitated speculation over solidarity, a private individualised world of greed over concern for the public world of social provision: put simply, a radical individualism over social interdependence.

The proponents of that economic worldview have not gone away. They remain, and their prescriptions are still at the heart of the politics of the Right. At most, such admission as they are willing to make is of a technical failure, of a miscalculation. They are obdurate in retaining reliance on a fundamental of their basic ideology – the suggested rational behaviour of disaggregated consumers in a market – as opposed to citizens with shared needs and vulnerabilities in a society. That is why the issue of who exercises state power remains important.

If there is need for a new politics and a new political economy, there is need also for a paradigm shift in the social sciences. The good news is that this is partially under way on the fringes of the different disciplines in the social sciences. Advanced thinking emerging from a new ecological awareness has been helpful in concentrating public awareness on the challenge posed by climate change. In the development area, in some feminist writing, and in cultural studies, the possible content of a different paradigm has to some extent been anticipated.

Sustainability contradicts radical unregulated market dominance. Historical and cultural factors reveal uneven development. Gender inclusion and participation challenge the social basis of demands in industry and agriculture. Yet very often these developments fail to address fundamental issues of power or the assumptions of the major structures of influence in society, and particularly of the state. They may end in advocating a simple form of communitarianism. This is to substitute a discourse on 'lifeboat' behaviour for the fundamental question as to why the ship is sinking even before the decision to abandon ship has been made.

An increasing awareness of shared global challenges – an awareness that has been made possible by a technological revolution in communications – is also posing a demand to all of the social sciences as we know them. We are coming to the end of simplistic dualism, of the Cartesian moment in intellectual thought. We have to recognise the diversity of our planet not only in a species sense, but also in terms of culture, memory and imagination. While the legacy of that moment which produced what has been called, in Western thought and society, the Enlightenment, shone a light on the necessity and possibilities of science, it has also betrayed us in ecological and social terms. The neglected connection between science, technology and society have exacted a heavy price.

The nineteenth-century idea of progress was followed by the mid-twentieth-century modernisation theory. These paradigms shared the common assumption of Western rational superiority. The result has been environmental degradation, unhealthy, unequal societies, and destructive poverty and exclusion.

Over the past number of years, and particularly since the election of President Obama, the importance of digital media has been highlighted. It has begun to change the political world, and politics has expanded to afford space to this new, fast-moving interface between politics, the public and technology. Technology, of course, can assist, but it can also cripple; it can go either way.

The developments in the technology of communications are both a challenge and an opportunity for political parties. 'Digital natives' – that is, those who from an early age have been immersed in the new technology and know no other life, and 'digital immigrants' –

are those who grew to maturity in the pre-internet age. As Marc Prensky puts it, writing of the Obama generation:

> Today's students represent the first generations to grow up with this new technology. They have spent their entire lives surrounded by and using computers, videogames, digital music players, video cameras, cell phones, and all the other toys and tools of the digital age. Today's average college graduates have spent less than 5,000 hours of their lives reading, but over 10,000 hours playing video games (not to mention 20,000 hours watching TV). Computer games, e-mail, the internet, cell phones and instant messaging are integral parts of their lives.
>
> So what should happen? Should the Digital Native students learn the old ways, or should their Digital Immigrant educators learn the new? Unfortunately, no matter how much the Immigrants may wish it, it is highly unlikely that the Digital Natives will go backwards. In the first place, it may be impossible – their brains may already be different. It also flies in the face of everything we know about cultural migration. Kids born into any new culture learn the new language easily, and forcefully resist using the old one. Smart adult immigrants *accept* that they do not know about their new world, and take advantage of their kids to help them learn and integrate. Not-so-smart (or not-so-flexible) immigrants spend most of their time grousing about how good things were in the 'old country'.

The issues which arise from the foregoing point to the intersection in history at which we have arrived. This intersection is of particular importance to a political party which, on the one hand, must retain contact with its history and traditions, to those things which gave rise to the party in question in the first instance – what gave it its raison d'être and values – and the need to harness new technology in order to disseminate its message and to touch new constituencies, new groupings of persons fluent in the new media.

It is important too, however, that the debate and the new kind of politics not be left, moored in the docks of technicism. It must include an appreciation of history and, for example, the tradition of utopianism which is a strong source of our own movement.

We should regard this new technical competence as a set of tools with which new initiatives in terms of policy and strategy can be built. It is not an either/or choice between such competence and a tradition of reading and activism that is assumed to lack such competence. We need both. We must ensure that every new development in technology is available for our political project, and we must prepare and adapt to achieve this.

On the other hand, however, a generation that was technically smart but without a political literacy, without familiarity or knowledge of the philosophy, history, values and unfinished project of the Left, would be of limited value. It could, indeed, be an obstacle, or constitute an embarrassing and shallow careerism. We need members with both a political vision and a technical competence. The capacity to change society requires courage and passion at times even more than skilful confidence.

The utopian tradition to which I have referred and which socialists draw on constitutes no idle dreaming. Ernst Bloch saw it as material that could be both transformative and emancipatory.

Ruth Levitas describes this in her response to Ernst Bloch's *The Principle of Hope*:

> The first English translation of *The Principle of Hope*, 1200 pages long, was published in 1986. It argues that the utopian impulse is an anthropological and ontological given, so that humankind constantly longs for a

better world. The sense of lack at the core of our existence can be articulated only through the projection of what would meet that lack, the delineation of what is missing. The utopian impulse, the impulse to a better world, is ubiquitous in human culture; but its expression is necessarily historically variable, and often oblique and fragmentary. Among the varied cultural forms that have a utopian content, Bloch discusses not just fairy tales and myths, but the alchemical quest for a process that will transmute base metal to gold; travellers' tales, such as St Brendan's voyage in search of the Promised Isles; and music and architecture. Bloch argues that there is a generic utopian content in these, a vital attempt to grasp the possibility of a radically different human experience, even though it is sometimes embedded in forms of fantasy that are easily dismissed as wishful thinking. For Bloch, wishful thinking is itself a precursor of wishful action, so this utopian content is indispensable. The appropriate analogy here is mining – extracting the utopian essence from the ore of human culture.

Tom Moylan, in the same work, made a powerful plea for a political engagement based on a utopian vision:

> *If*, then, utopian justice and fulfilment are to be lived by all, what is needed, in this new century as in other times, is a courageous embrace of the utopian project, not self-denying resignation but self-aware engagement. As this volume, and this essay, argues, however, the political work of utopian transformation requires the (theorised) knowledge of its dangers *and* its opportunities, its negative and positive tendencies. If, and when, a political movement is again carried forward or a better social order is successfully established, the subversive

and creative-utopian energy of the project at each and
every moment must be protected within the problem-
atic practices that inform and drive it. To prevent closure and privilege – or at least to enable successful challenges to any such that develop – the conditions for a
renewable utopian function must be made available.
Thus – along with these senses of Utopia's strength and
its temporary duration – another important element in
the utopian method is *memory*, in particular that form
of memory that is productive rather than consoling or
disempowering.

Language itself, too, can betray us as easily as serve our emancipatory project. We need to redefine our terms, for example, in
speaking of the economy. A practical example from the world of
work is perhaps useful. We have come to expect a definition of wage
income that was exclusively based on the traded economy. Work in
the caring area, in voluntary activity, in cultural activity, while taking time and effort, most importantly commitment, was accorded a
lesser status. The new paradigm of work will require a recognition
of such effort. The caring economy has to be recognised as part of
the social economy. Income issues that facilitate or obstruct citizenship are more important than the debate on wages and competitiveness.

If we are politically challenged to state where we stand on the
future of the economy, we must realise that buried in that challenge
is the frequent media suggestion that we must get back to where we
were a decade ago. Such a project is not merely insufficient in dealing with our present crisis; it is unacceptable. What it suggests is a
resuscitation of something that has failed. The consequence of
unregulated neo-liberal market economics is that so many lives are
in ruins not just in Ireland but in Europe and the entire world. It is

inescapable therefore for Labour as a party of the Left that it specify a new form of the economy, a social economy.

We have to remember, however, that given electoral events in Europe, the response in several countries, indeed the majority of countries, in terms of economic polity, will be to follow the prescription of the Right, to adjust the citizenry to the demands of a restricted and crippled market through cuts in benefit and the withdrawal of services.

The Left must oppose this development. However, the role of the Left must not be just to oppose this consciously created extension of poverty. We are required to outline the shape of the alternative. We have to achieve a shift in consciousness among the public, give intellectual leadership, create confidence through education and organisation. All this represents a very great challenge.

The neo-liberal moment in Europe was made possible by acceptance at a general level of the suggestion that its version of the market economy was inevitable, even natural. This became an axiom of media truth and was also regarded in certain academic circles as a truth that could be imposed through financial, even developmental, policy on the poorest peoples of the world. It was what we might call the high moment of that Cartesian hubris to which I referred earlier: a Western moment of rational achievement that had to be forced on backward peoples.

The new economics and the new policies must draw on a wider and richer cultural basis. The collective character of economics must be restored. That which has failed has been based on the principle that the economic impulse is inherently individualistic. Much more than the rejection of solidarity, there is an aggression associated with this view. If, as far back as Francis Bacon, imperialism and colonisation combined to destroy cultures and nature itself, in the contemporary world grinding poverty creates insecurity and is the basis frequently of conflict. If we are to avoid new massive sustained and widespread conflict, we have to engage with the necessary components of modern citizenship. We have to build the subject of economics anew. We have to seek a mandate for a social, sustainable, inter-generationally responsible set of economic policies.

I repeat, there is an intellectual and academic background to our present crisis. The present economic crisis, with its misery of nearly thirty million unemployed people in Europe, the prospect of half a million unemployed people in Ireland, and half of the people on the planet living in abject poverty, is the fruit of a particular model of the connection between economy and society – radical individualism.

It is worth recalling the injunction of Friedrich von Hayek, the high-priest of radical market theory. His view was that the market order was beyond human comprehension, but necessary:

> The aim of the market order is to cope with the inevitable ignorance of everybody, of most of the particular facts which determine this order. By a process which men did not understand, their activities have produced an order much more extensive and comprehensive than anything that could comprehend it, but on the functions of which we have become utterly dependent.

It has been one of the weaknesses of the Left that it has not drawn on the richness of its own utopian inheritance. It is, I believe, one of the defining differences between the politics of the Right and the Left that the Left believes in the possibility of creating a truly human society with the economy viewed as instrumental to that end. Again, too, the Left can be expected to argue for the defence and enhancement of the public world and the citizen's role within it: the creation of a real and meaningful citizenship.

We are entering a period in which the contest must be made clear between the politics of the Left and the politics of the Right. While we must take heart from an increasing awareness of the threat posed by climate change, we must also face the failure to create a sufficient awareness as to the price being paid for inequality at every level on our planet. Unequal societies are more likely to be unhealthy societies than societies with egalitarian policies.

I have referred elsewhere to the consequences of an increasingly monopolised media that narrowed political and economic discourse in such a way as to blind people as to the enormous levels, not just of inequality but of monopoly that it tolerated. I quoted Adam Hanieh, who in his essay in *The New Imperialists* wrote:

> Look at the food sector: five companies control 90 percent of the world's grain trade, six companies control 80 percent of the world pesticide market, three companies control 85 percent of the world's tea market, two companies control 50 percent of the world trade in bananas, three companies control almost 80 percent of the confectionery market, four companies control 75 percent of the retail trade in the UK. In media and entertainment, nine large conglomerates dominate the sector, with five companies controlling about 80 percent of the music industry worldwide.

That is but one example of the world of von Hayek, of Thatcher, of Reagan, of Charlie McCreevy, of all the apostles of the politics of the Right.

That world was supported by an economics that was far from neutral. It was really amoral. Its basic premise was that the only true freedom was a freedom based on rational individualistic choice allowed for by a completely unregulated market. The only freedom given recognition was the freedom to infinitely increase one's consumption. At times, freedom of the market, à la Milton Friedman, was sought to be imposed at the cost of political freedom itself.

The present international banking crisis is of course also a cameo of what is irrational. The destruction in recent times of the banking system in the United States, with its horrific consequences for the world economy, was based on an insatiable greed on several levels. At the lowest level, house owners were encouraged to purchase homes at inflated prices, keep them for a while, and then, with further indebtedness, continue moving up the ladder of a fictional home-ownership existence. Wall Street demanded new mortgage-related products, which became the seed for debt-based bogus products, which were given triple-A recommendations by ratings agencies that were themselves conflicted.

The greed was unlimited. Otto Scharmer, in a recent lecture, tells us that the top 50 in the finance houses took incomes of $590 million per person in 2007, and indeed, even after the collapse of the financial system in the United States, $18 billion of President Obama's financial package again went in compensation to the heads of financial houses. Neither they nor their political friends have gone away.

It has to be accepted that the restructuring of the real economy cannot be assigned to being a mere residual consequence of banking stability. Our central-bank surpluses should be used for an employment-creating stimulus.

Again, before we deflate the economy further, by restricting, through indiscriminate levies, the incomes of those carrying the greatest burden, we should eliminate the speculative property-based tax breaks that contributed to our crisis, and indeed go further and seek a clawback through short- and medium-term levies on dead and unproductive wealth.

A recovered economy can create conditions for fiscal stability and ensure a transparent, accountable banking system that serves citizens. The real economy and the security it serves must be given priority before it is too late, before a huge burden of toxic bank debt is dumped on future generations as well as the present ones.

Priority has to be given to getting activity in the real economy – an economy that includes recognising social contributions, the capacity of the creative space in our society, and the immense opportunities that are presented by a responsible approach to the challenges of climate change and sustainability.

We must seek a partnership for reform in the public service that respects the motivation and commitment of those who work in the public service. We must use that partnership to create a common project built on the aim of achieving a better form of citizenship – one that is based on a mutual respect and that allows appropriate discretion, combined with total transparency. The huge gaps within the public service, often based on hierarchy and patriarchy, have to be addressed so as to make it a positive and exciting career to work to serve the public in a diversity of ways in a creative society that respects all citizens as equal.

Above all else, we must refuse to translate our unemployment levels into a form of forced inactivity. We cannot turn massive cyclical unemployment into long-term unemployment. We have therefore to examine a myriad of ways of creating opportunities for experience, placement, upskilling and retraining. We should also look at redesigning and redefining work, in terms of time and space, and at work-sharing. Our traditional approach to unemployment promises nothing more than increasing misery in an overstretched, bureaucratic setting.

The Labour Party was never more relevant than today, and our work will go on. Our challenge, amongst others, goes beyond the arena of elected politicians and politics – although this is a crucial location, since it is the space at which the public gaze is directed – but our work must encompass energy and vitality in other areas also.

We must have clearly recognisable emancipatory policies that are understood, and have the enthusiastic support of all our members and supporters. We must be a party of agitation, a party that campaigns energetically, and a party, too, which continues to make its case to the people and to seek their support.

We must invite those interested in our mission to join with us in seeking to make Ireland, and a world which we all share, spaces which deliver a version of our common shared humanity, a humanity no longer defiled by an extreme version of individualism, greed and destructive capitalism. We must know why it is important for ourselves and others to be of the Left, and proud to be of Labour.

Address to Tom Johnson Summer School, Galway,
5 July 2009

9.

Restoring Ethics to Politics and Economics

Responding to our Global Interdependency

May I begin by saying that many people today experience a great longing for authenticity. They sense that at a personal, community, and global level they have experienced a frustration at best, perhaps even a violence that condemns them and others to a life far short of their capacities at an ethical or creative level. Such a strong statement is one that is very particular to this present age, but it is one that has engaged scholarship at different periods in different centuries in a powerful way. For example, there is a particular moment when the spiritual gives way to the rational, and the Enlightenment arrives. There is a particular moment when modernism arrives, but what one can detect in the present period is a deep search for authenticity and a sense of frustration at what is not being realised in real economic terms.

One of the distinguishing characteristics of the present time is that there is a greater intolerance for the discussion of such a contradiction, and such a problem, than at any time since I started as a student or as a university teacher. It is a time of narrowness. It is a time of extreme intolerance and it is, to my mind, a time of a very reduced scholarship. Recent statements by current and retired heads of third-level institutions give cause for the greatest concern. Such statements seem to advocate little less than the destruction of the limited capacity for critical scholarship that exists. The agenda being advocated is an intolerant imposition of a neo-utilitarian philosophy that has neither been examined nor subjected to critique. It is a miserable view of the world and of learning.

I am suggesting that we cannot live fully conscious lives unless we question the inevitabilities that are suggested to us. This involves developing both the personal consciousness and social consciousness that is necessary to create a critical capacity, so that we might truly experience freedom and choice, and moral responsibility for the consequences of our actions. Second, I suggest that in dealing with that kind of challenge, we will find no automatic solution in retreating to old certainties. This does not mean that the certainties have been discarded. I am simply suggesting, philosophically, that they are insufficient. For example, I was a young student in the United States, Britain and Ireland in the 1960s and into the 1970s, when we were told that the Western World was an advanced world, and it was a matter of time until the rest of the planet lost its backwardness and could become modern and developed, just like us. The fact was, of course, that this set of assumptions constituted a model that was ethnocentric. As a model it was culturally insufficient, and in sociological terms as a theory of change, unacceptable in its assumptions, its methodology, and above all in its conclusions. It was also historically not very credible – a fact that didn't seem to bother many people. It spawned a host of works, and a kind of scholarship that was unilinear, evolutionist, and accepting of political and economic structures that were in political, economic and cultural terms dominating, exploitive and manipulative.

Turning to the necessity to question inevitabilities and the certainties that are not sufficient to deal with this angst of our times, people change beliefs, and have done so in the history of ideas, through the constructions of myths. The nature of a myth is such that you suggest that something is so obvious that it is natural for it to be taken for granted – rather like modernisation, was a myth. It was a powerful myth. There was no person who studied at postgraduate level in the United States in that period from the end of the 1960s to the end of the 1980s who wasn't reared within this myth. Globalisation is a contemporary related myth.

When you look at the assumptions of globalisation – that you have a single model of the economy to be prosecuted in a linear way, market-led and so forth, private- rather than public-driven, with no notion of involvement of the state and unmitigated by social protection – one can see that globalisation too is a myth. The difference between it and the modernisation myth is that it is being implemented through institutions which were not originally set up for such a purpose, such as the IMF, and, although there is a crucial difference between them, the World Bank. Joseph Stiglitz has critiqued that difference between the IMF and the World Bank, but it is a myth. The difference between such a myth and others is that it is a dangerous myth. Where it is most dangerous is that it dulls critical capacity.

In relation to my opening statement, that we experience a longing for authenticity, consciousness tells us that it doesn't matter enormously where it is institutionally located, simply that spirit cries out for a version of the self and of the world, and for the capacity for creation, that is not being met by our present circumstances. We have to answer that problem through an integrated scholarship that is not so easily available to us any more. It is as if we try to see these problems through a broken glass, through pieces and shards of experience. Thinking it through raises a question about the role of culture – culture which is at once inherited and being recreated, but also fundamentally charged, never static. Creativity is not something that is located randomly and vicariously in individual people, like that lovely phrase about 'She had it in her', or 'The piano will stand to her', or whatever. The alternative view is that we are all, and all children in particular are, potentially creative, if they are allowed to develop. Genius may be more randomly and vicariously distributed.

Accepting the necessity and power of creativity has implications for our discourse on the economy. I have been at many conferences on the knowledge economy; I repeat something that I have taken to repeating in the hope that it would lodge somewhere. It is that the creative society makes possible myriad forms of the knowledge economy, but if you change the society to one form of the knowledge economy in a period of time, you not only damage your capacity economically, but you dislocate the creative society and you diminish the capacity for a vibrant citizenship.

This is something that has to be taken seriously because it has wider implications, such as the relationship of education to the economy at every level through the economy. If today you state that you are, as an academic, in favour of reflective scholarship, this somehow or other is to confess a disability in the current times in relation to funding. I was an academic for most of my life. I have taught in the university system, in America, in Britain, and here in Ireland. I am distressed at what I see as this lack of confidence in the possibility of hope at an intellectual level.

In previous decades, scholars seemed so much more morally engaged. If I were to go back to Jung's work in 1933, before World War II, scholars were trying to envisage a time where we would never have war again. Then, through the sixties and seventies, an immense debate arose about what you might call the enframing of technology and science. There was a debate about the bomb. There was a debate about the use of physicists in creating instruments of war, about whether or not science was neutral, and of its relationship to technology.

The story, of course, is not a black one entirely. One of the greatest developments through the last twenty-five years has been an increasing interest in ecological responsibility. Even at the UN Conference at Rio, you had the Business Council for Sustainable Development deciding that sustainable development was an unavoidable concept.

Looking back at the origins of a dangerous hubris, the high point of an uncaring science was perhaps when Francis Bacon said: 'I lead to you Nature and all her children in bondage for your use', and again on nature, 'We must gouge out her secrets'. Francis Bacon, at the beginning of a period of empire and colonisation, was supplying a rationalisation for these forces, and a relationship to the environment which would be tragic in its consequences. It was not accidental that such views on nature were sited in the movement towards the establishment of colonisation and empire. These constituted a frame of mind, a paradigm, a governing myth. So we are searching, therefore, for a new paradigm in which we might enframe science and technology, and at the same time discover, or rediscover, points of continuity from the past and culture and be able to face the future without fear.

One of the most important aspects of change in our contemporary lives has been the change in the relationship between economy and society. Our attitude to work and leisure has been crucially changed. A new discourse has been invented to justify our subservience to the economy. Issues of personal and social development have given way to ones of utility. We rarely hear such questions as 'What would you really like to do with your life? Where do you think your interests really lie?' On the other hand, we are instructed on a daily basis as to what we must do with our lives and our children's lives to sustain 'the needs of the economy'.

Our society is under pressure for time. Voluntarism is declining. There is little time for community. Time previously spent with neighbours is spent in traffic jams. We earn more, but everything costs even more. The relationship between the generations is fundamentally changed, with care of the elderly, for example, now being discussed almost entirely in terms of institutional provision. We have 65.1 percent above average of women now in the Irish workforce, and we have 1.5 percent of people above the age of sixty-five. There is hardly anybody else to be sent to the economy.

If you contrast the present discourse to that which prevailed when I was appointed first in 1969 in University College Galway, as it then was, we were being endlessly invited to attend seminars about the leisure society. What were we all going to do when there was so much free time? Take on hobbies, learn languages, travel? People were to prepare themselves for retirement. I remember quoting Oscar Wilde's phrase 'work is for horses'. The working life was to be shorter. The working year was to be shorter. The working day was to be shorter. Then suddenly there was no free time. Now it is a disloyal and near-traitorous act not to work endlessly. You are letting the economy down if you retire at seventy! For young couples, there is only so much time left after you have a massive increase in the social time demanded by going to work and coming back, and demanded by both partners.

A solution to our form of economy has to be structured across the spectrum of space and time. It has to take into account the issues of income but also issues of quality of life. The challenge is to sustain the version that you want of the economy, and at the same time make any progress towards that which I have been describing in terms of realising your ethically unrealised selves.

We began most of our lives when the concept of citizenship was being widely debated. With citizenship came notions of universal rights. Surely people should be entitled to clean water? Surely people should be entitled to education? Surely people should be entitled to good housing? Surely people should be free from insecurity in illness or in old age? But now we listen to lectures about how we should purchase our own security in every one of these areas. We are becoming consumers of services that will more and more be provided to us by the market rather than as rights we are entitled to under a concept of citizenship. The same French company that provides water to those of the black community in California is providing it in South Africa. In fairness to the South African government, they are trying to get them out and get back to some concept of public provision.

Such a world as I have described has been accepted as our inevitable world. This world, sustained by the myth of globalisation, is a world about which we have to ask ourselves a fundamental question. Do we have the critical capacity to subject it to critique? We have in our consciousness actually shifted to being consumers rather than citizens. This is accompanied by the commodification of more and more aspects of life, and it has created an alienation that has masked itself as a sole desirable lifestyle – a lifestyle that invites us, I suggest, towards a life of being consumed in one's consumption. The interdependency which was at the basis of citizenship is recognised, but it is devalued by an aggressive and indeed, I suggest, at times a vicious individualism. Indeed, I notice that our language itself has changed. People rarely speak about 'the personal' any more, but speak instead of 'the individual'.

Market fundamentalism, I have suggested, is accepted as the single paradigm of economic development, and its imposition as the sole strategy for development and poverty alleviation. This, I suggest, is disastrous – and not only in the poorest countries, or transition economies, but also in the so-called developed world is this so.

We have as consumers experienced such a dulling of our consciousness as blocks our capacity to critically engage with our world. For example, if we take the media as an example, we are affected by fragmentation of audiences, concentration of ownership, and a drive towards cultural homogeneity. We should be honest and accept that the concentration of ownership in the media internationally, with its stress on commoditised entertainment on television in particular, plays a crucial role in this limitation, even destruction, of our life-world.

Our scholarship has become apologetic and accommodating rather than critical. We are, as Charles Taylor, the Canadian philosopher, puts it: 'acquiescing in our own unfreedom'. We are 'drifting', as he puts its, to our 'unfreedom'.

This broken world appears to us in shadows through the shards of experience; some of the most insightful and ethical responses that do engage with this condition, do so on a single-issue basis. I found, for example – and this is even more controversial – that some of my friends, who **became communitarians** in the eighties, in California, did not want a strong role for the state, the bureaucracy. Let's all do it – make the changes – from the bottom up. Ronald Reagan, as governor, clasped his hands and said thank you for helping me. He closed the parks. Nettles grew where flowers grew before. Some well-meaning reformers had assisted the agenda of the Right without thinking about it.

Again, one of the fastest areas for growth in bookshops, not only here but all over Europe, and particularly in North America, is self-healing books. This raises the question: can you heal yourself? The answer in such writing is of course that you must heal yourself first, and then you get on to the continent, and then to the world. I suggest that much of this is a very insufficient response to the kind of problems I have been describing. Of course, it is important to recognise the importance of personal integration so as to survive in a broken world, but we need to attend to the urgency of an integrated approach to our common shared interdependent planetary existence. We have, to invert a Raymond Williams phrase, become the targets of consumption rather than the arrows of a deeper, more extensive and humane communication. We have the technological capacity to widen and deepen our communication and engage with all the issues of the world and with other people from different cultures. Instead of such a project, the technology has been turned against us.

Even in the production values of television programmes, context is eliminated and a distrust of narrative is obvious. There is a distrust of the possibility of democratic extension. The world, in the new value system, is one whose complexity is amenable solely to expertise. The view it sustains is that such an expertise is separate from ordinary democratic discourse. Ordinary people, it is suggested, do not understand. From this assumption, it is a short distance to the dangerous views of Leo Strauss, with the notion that the public may have to be deceived, and the concept of the 'noble lie', as adopted by the neo-conservatives in the recent history of the United States.

It is appropriate to ask the question as to what kind of world we inhabit. Why do we accept it? What are the consequences of appearing to recognise an interdependency that we are forced to contradict? As we discard ethics for a narrow market fundamentalism, can social cohesion survive? In Mrs Thatcher's Britain, one of the fastest growth areas was in private security firms. You had very wealthy homes in gated communities, which they felt they needed for protection because of their perception that the underclass was coming up the road and, as the new rich from Mrs Thatcher's spec-ulative economy put it: 'they want what we have, and we are pro-tecting ourselves against them, because we know what they want, and they are not getting it'.

The acceptance of a world so divided, a planet that is not suffi-ciently respected for its diversity, places much at risk. It has a numb-ing effect. People regularly say to me that they are not happy about this or that, and they want to do something about it, but they lack the moral resources and the courage to actually debate it. All I want at the present time is to simply raise some questions that I feel to be important, but that are neglected.

Going back to Jung's work, he spoke about the unconscious, and then about the practical consciousness that enabled one to do tasks but, more importantly, of a discursive consciousness, which was one where you allowed yourself to ask the questions: Why am I doing this? What are the reasons behind this?

Jung gave the example of people in the Western World in the past when they went to continents like Africa, finding it to be so absurd that people believed that if you shoot an animal and an old woman dies in a neighbouring village, you have robbed her soul. The Western visitors thought that such a notion was ridiculous. Yet it was only 'natural' to be overdressed in the tropical heat, to require one's servants to wear white gloves over their black hands.

So there is a problem about what is natural. That phrase – what is natural – purports to describe what is inevitable and purports to make the myths by which we might live. I have been to many places where there are huge problems with poverty, disease and malnutrition. The question digs itself into you. How often do we have to see this and experience it again and again on television? Doesn't it really contradict any ethical or moral impulse we claim to have with us, when we insist that many things repeat themselves as if they were inevitable.

In 1994, the late and brilliant Erskine Childers, who was an assistant general secretary of the United Nations, wrote in his book *Renewing the United Nations*: '1.4 billion people now live in absolute poverty – 40 percent more than fifteen years ago. Nearly one in every four human beings alive today is only existing on the margins of survival, too poor to obtain the food they need to work, or adequate shelter, or minimal health care, let alone education for their children', then he said, 'overall for the poorest among humankind, the thirty years . . . between sixty-four and ninety-four have been like trying to go up a down escalator'.

In 2000, the international community appeared to respond to what Erskine Childers had noted. It adopted what became known as the World Millennium Goals, which were to be achieved by 2015. These eight goals can be summarised as follows:

1. The reduction by half of those living in poverty and hunger by 2015;
2. The achievement of universal primary education;
3. The elimination of gender disparity in primary and secondary education by 2005 and at all levels by 2015;
4. The reduction of child mortality of under-fives by two-thirds;
5. The education of the maternal mortality ratio by three-quarters;
6. The halting of the spread of HIV/AIDs, TB, measles and malaria;
7. The ending of environmental degradation and the achievement of a sustainable environment;
8. The creation of a fair global partnership for development.

Here is how Jeffrey Sachs summarises the impact the achievement of these goals would have, were they to be achieved. If the Millennium Goals were achieved between 2005 and 2015:

- 500 million people would be lifted out of extreme poverty;
- 300 million people would no longer suffer from hunger;
- 350 million fewer people would lack access to clean water;
- 650 million people would have greater access to sanitation;
- 30 million children who would otherwise have died would be alive;
- the lives of 2 million women who would have died in child-birth would be saved.

The achievement of the Millennium Development Goals represents, I suggest, the greatest moral challenge of our time. It is a challenge in which the international community is failing.

The existing structures of aid, trade and debt – the neo-liberal market model imposed on us – promises failure in the achievement of these goals and assures us not just of the continuity of existing divisions but of these divisions being deepened, and fissures opening up based on access to information technology.

In 1960, the richest one-fifth of the world's population enjoyed thirty times more than the income of the poorest fifth. By 1989, the richest fifth was receiving sixty times the income of the poorest. As to the areas of aid, trade and debt, in relation to aid, aid has been falling every year for the last ten years. In relation to trade, what is being transferred from the South to the North every day remains unfair. I say this in relation to debt. If debt had been cancelled in 1997, for the twenty poorest countries, the money released for basic health care could have saved the lives of about 21 million children; by 2000, the equivalent of 19,000 children per day.

To give an example from one African country, Zambia in 1989 paid in debt service a sum that was 13 percent of its gross domestic product. It was greater than the combined health and education budget. For every 1 percent you transferred from debt service to the combined health education product, you would have been able to save the lives of children at the level I have mentioned. In that country, life expectancy due to HIV and AIDs has fallen from forty-three years to thirty-three years, with half a million children out of school and the education system in a state of collapse.

If we were to seriously think about reform of policies in relation to aid, trade debt and technology transfer, we already have an agenda which started in September 2000 through the eight Millennium Development Goals, about which there should not be any backsliding. At the present time, one of the eight millennium goals – that which deals with Africa and HIV and AIDs – is at about 42 percent of what is required. This is less than half of the money committed in Johannesburg, and it is something like $42 billion short of what is needed to redress that problem.

It is sometimes suggested that aid and debt relief should not be given to countries that do not meet certain standards in relation to the elimination of corruption. In this regard, it is important to be even-handed and to let the light shine on the full house of corruption. Recently, I announced a campaign for the ratification and implementation of the United Nations Convention Against Corruption.

The elimination of corruption is an important part of the development agenda. To date, however, the debate has suffered from being one-sided. While it is appropriate that receiving countries should be scrutinised, there has been a comprehensive silence on the part of many on the activities of the multinational corporations and the international banking system, which have been sourcing and processing acts of corruption on a grand scale.

Ratification of the Convention will enable the recovery of funds stolen from people by corrupt leaders and lodged in the international banking system. There is a good precedent upon which to build. For example, $700 million was recovered to Nigeria from the Swiss banking system – money stolen by the late President Abacha. This required negotiations between the government of Nigeria and the government of Switzerland. These actions need to multiply.

The debate on corruption has indeed been one-sided. At times its one-sided character has impacted negatively on the generosity of donors and their willingness to contribute to much-needed international aid and debt relief.

Ratification of the UN Convention Against Corruption is the way to do this. Article 51 of the Convention, for example, provides for the return of assets as a fundamental principle, and Article 43 provides for the most general cooperation between countries.

Ireland cannot afford to delay any longer on ratification, and indeed, the European Union has lost credibility for its prescriptions on good governance by its failure to ratify. Ireland should not only ratify but should urge ratification on its fellow members of the European Union who have not done so.

I have written to all the Irish-based NGOs asking for their support on the matter. This is an issue of great importance, and I am hoping for support for all quarters for what I believe may be a significant and necessary initiative.

In conclusion, may I suggest the following about our acceptance of the current received versions of our contemporary world, with its single, hegemonic version of neo-liberal economics: if we had wanted to live fully conscious critical lives, if we had wanted not to be the target, if we had wanted not to have the arrows directed at us, as consumers, if we had wanted, as Raymond Williams put it, to be the arrow not the target, would we have accepted so much of the monopoly I mentioned earlier in the media?

Between 1987 and 1989, that very mobile man, when it comes to citizenship, Mr Rupert Murdoch, through his News

Corporation, earned $2.3 billion. He paid no corporation tax, and in the whole world, for all his operations, he paid less than six percent tax. Do we regard that as a good thing? Why do so many secretly admire such people? Why do people put up with all this inequality and poverty?

There is a suggestion being promulgated in our society, and often disseminated from positions of privilege, such as non-executive board membership, or leadership in third-level institutions, that occasionally, through some kind of individual miracle, or more usually through embracing the extreme versions of individualism, all of humanity can escape from the condition of poverty. Such speeches are usually made in contexts where no critique or reply is possible.

What is needed is a return to questioning the inevitabilities by which we live, looking, perhaps, at some of the certainties that have been discarded, without replacement, and critiquing the myths by which we live, concentrating on the critical capacity that the scholarship requires and that public debate requires, encouraging consciousness, respecting prophesies.

We still retain the wonderful capacity to imagine and realise a world that can be created, can yet be made to happen, that we can make our own history. But we should recall perhaps one of the most inspiring phrases written by Raymond Williams in his last book, *Towards 2000*: 'Once the inevitabilities are challenged, we have begun to gather our resources for a journey of hope.' Once the inevitabilities of our times are challenged, we have taken our first steps towards a new world, and hope made manifest dissolves our fear.

Address at Labour Youth Conference, NUI Galway, 2005

10.

Citizenship:
The Space of Politics Recovered

One of the most discernible trends in contemporary society is the acceptance of a view of politics, society and the economy as separated out from each other. A mechanistic pseudo-rationality governs an economic discourse that is perceived as having nothing to do with social critique or a discourse of ethics.

No longer does the phrase 'political economy' find usage in policy discourse. Thus, poverty is seen as an aspect of social policy unhinged from economic policy.

Politics is devalued. It is seen as having lost public trust, and the view of it propagated by various trends is negative. Individual participants, in their silent fear of populism, feed the stereotypical view of corruption created by a few.

This facilitates a new ultra-conservative view that the economy must be freed from political direction and left to find its own level. This is to be driven by a free market which is assumed to be beneficial despite the obtrusive presence of monopolistic tendencies and an unrestrained concentration of ownership, which is delivering a new economic exploitation.

The demand for the removal of decision-making in the political sphere on levels of public expenditure, on pay for the lower paid, or on borrowing, are examples of the new 'unaccountable' economics: an economics that regards the public as a mere component of a self-regulating economic system. This is a profoundly ideological position. At the same time, politics itself is reduced to a contest of competing populisms.

From such a broken linkage between the economy and politics comes a society that is characterised by fragmentation, alienation and disillusionment.

An obvious extension of the individualism of the marketplace is the privatisation of experience. If, in the past, citizens agitated in the public space for rights to participate in the state, the society and the economy, now it is as consumers that they are asked to calculate in a private space. It is not from the power of citizens that demands surface, but from the demands of consumers interfaced with the market.

We are drifting to a final rupture between the economy, politics and society. If this happens, the ensuing conflict will not be mediated through trade unions, political parties or social movements. It will be a naked confrontation between, on the one side, the wealthy getting wealthier, and the poor getting poorer; between the excluded and the powerful; between the technologically sophisticated and the technologically manipulated. It will be a conflict as raw as any in the history of private accumulation between, on the one hand, consumers, and, on the other, the excluded poor, who no longer have any norms of citizenship that they share or which would mediate their conflict.

Public participation is now falling in every institution of civil society. The norms of a shared life have little opportunity of being articulated. That is the inescapable other side of the coin of globalisation, which is the unaccountable economy on a world scale. That is why it is necessary for the Left to outline the case for a new and vibrant citizenship that can vindicate such values as solidarity, community, democracy, justice, freedom and equality. These values can be achieved by giving them a practical expression in a new theory of citizenship.

Citizenship generates rights and thoughts that are shared and respected. The life of the person is respected as having a value that is enhanced as a shared public value beyond the narrow consumption power of the individual.

Citizenship thus requires universality of provision of basic needs in income, health, housing, social welfare, education and culture. Because the society is organised on the basis of citizenship, the minimum provision which facilitates participation, inclusion, freedom, personal development and celebration is viewed as a matter of rights.

The practical achievement of this goal must guide a left-of-centre government's policies. For example, education must be accessible, and democratic in structure; a citizen is entitled to such. He or she is not simply a consumer seeking to purchase a private commodity: again, workers have rights as a workforce to organise and participate in the economy and society in a way that is beyond the personal assertion of economic and social rights.

In every area of policy, a theory of citizenship is relevant. As the economy grows, it requires that all citizens be enabled to participate in that growth. More importantly, it stresses that the purpose of growth is the improvement in the welfare of the citizenry. It is necessary, too, to end the myth that any redistributive measures are inimical to economic growth. There is real evidence that the opposite can be the case.

In areas of justice, an active theory of citizenship builds bonds of security that stand in stark contrast to purchased safety from a society feared as endemically crime-ridden. Responsible politics has to develop an understanding of deviance, a critique of law, and a spectrum of care, as well as social control.

The information society now being created is one where we can utilise technology to serve citizens, to enable them to communicate and participate as never before with benefit to themselves and society, or we can abandon the technology to the marketplace to create new classes of the information-rich and the information-poor, of the literate and the illiterate, of the participating and the excluded.

The choice is clear: citizenship created with a democratic agenda, socially inclusive, politically accountable, with an economy viewed as instrumental, or on the other hand a populist consumerism where rights are defined by purchasing power, where society is viewed as a conflict zone, and the political system is construed as a place of corruption.

Progressive policies must derive from a belief in citizenship restated through the values of the Left in new conditions of modernity. We must offer a politics that is active, inclusive, ethical and just. It is the greatest and most exciting challenge at the beginning of a new century: building a democratic citizenship in a just economy and an actively participative civil society.

If we believe in a democratic citizenship recast, we must stand for the right of every citizen to participate in society with the opportunity to develop their personal and social selves in conditions of freedom, communal solidarity, justice and equality.

The Labour Party, since its foundation before that of the State itself, has stood for a version of society that was built on these values. It must re-articulate them. Labour, given its history and internationalism, has a particular role to play in any debate on citizenship.

The past of a political party might be constituted as a narrative. This lends itself to drawing on the roots and history of a political party; not merely as a source, or validation, of past struggle, but, much more importantly, as a source of renewal in terms of the basic values of the political party or movement in question.

It is not, however, a narrative that is written in stone. It has to be flexible. History demands that it be such. Fundamental values have to be restated and recast to deal with new circumstances and challenges. Again, the narrative has to envisage the shape of the future. This latter is an exercise of imagination. It also, crucially, requires the shape of the narrative of the future, the alternative narrative, to be made manifest. It has to be articulated.

Beyond such articulation there is a need to connect the values and principles at its heart with the political discourse of the day. This requires the conversion of the narrative into policy around which the mobilisation of support can be sought.

Labour must see our history as the shared stories of our diverse experience. It sees the history of working people, of women and minorities, as an example to its movement, even if these stories were excluded in conservative history. Today Labour must give voice to the emerging stories of those who are dominated, excluded, oppressed and exploited; and regard them as its heritage.

Deriving its values from a history of struggle for democracy, Labour seeks to establish the same conditions of freedom, communal solidarity, justice and equality in contemporary society. Thus it is not only Labour's drawing from a tradition of struggle for these values that makes it different. It is Labour's restating of these values in new conditions that makes it different to other parties today.

The inescapable task for Labour and the Left is one of putting their core values before the people. It also requires us to respect the freedom of imagination, to be creative. The Left must exercise freedom as well as demanding it.

We should see our citizens as sharing and using the economy

and technology to achieve their values. We should see the people as the makers of history, not as its passive victims. We should see them as the creators of forms of history, not its pawns. Above all, we should see the public and those yet to be born as creators of forms of human society, more ethical, more just, and more communal than has been either experienced or envisaged to date.

Such a view of citizenship might lead, for example, to a theory of the media that is active rather than passive. In the introduction of digitalisation, for example, citizens' ability to communicate and learn takes precedence over market services.

Again, in urban planning, citizens' use of the safe public space would be assured over minimal concessions from a speculative market.

In every area, be it health, education or justice, to name but three, it is possible to give a citizenship policy proposal which would be different from other managerial models because it is traced from a theory and process of citizenship rights.

Citizenship policies thus create an agenda of rights and responsibilities. Europe has yet to create a Europe of citizens. The concept, therefore, has local, national and European application. If the EU is to be a Europe of citizens, it will have to reintegrate politics and economics. It will have to put globalisation into accountable practice and discourse.

The alternative, of fitting consumers to the global market, is a recipe for violence that could inevitably accompany the collapse of political discourse as we know it, and indeed the rejection of ethics and politics as sources of guiding principles in life, as society itself succumbs to an unaccountable market.

11.

Culture, Creativity, Community and the Creative Industries

The debate currently under way as to the relationship between creativity, culture and the economy, and the consequences such relationships may have for citizenship, is of fundamental import-ance. It is a debate that raises core issues as to democracy itself, the participation of citizens, the quality of life, and the nature of human activity in general and work in particular.

In recent times, the discourse has reflected the fact that so many economies are in recession. What were previously policy discussions about the arts, about cultural policy, have changed into fascinating projections as to the economic value of what are now called the creative industries.

Within this definition of creative industries lie the traditional practices of the arts, but in the transition from arts, through culture, to creative industries, not only has the net of what is included been extended, but there is a tendency to discuss what was previously a cultural matter, or even a citizenship matter, as something that can be appropriately considered by existing economic measures. It is as if within the cultural space, a *terra nova* of the creative industries has suddenly been discovered. This raises of course the issue as to whether we are seeking to build a strong cultural space, enabling creativity to emerge within it, for citizens in general and for people of all ages, or are we alternatively colonising a previously relatively free space of human activity for the economic benefit of the few rather than the many.

There is of course an alternative view, one that suggests that we must seek to straddle both these options. A recent article by Heather McClean describes such an exercise in the city of Toronto. In her account of the debates for the mayoralty of Toronto in 2010, she presents a fascinating account of the presentations of three of the four front-running mayoral candidates: Rocco Rossi, George Smitherman and Joe Pantalone. All three offered proposals which she described as 'neo-liberal urban policies celebrating the mythical ideal of an artistic and inclusive, yet competitive and business-friendly 'creative city':

> The creative city script is a 'third way' policy model for urban politicians followed closely by the outgoing Toronto Mayor David Miller and left-leaning city council: it glosses over competitive market-friendly policies with a sophisticated, urbane and progressive veneer – neo-liberalism with a hip and urban face.

The fourth candidate, Rob Ford, had a view that the arts community was swallowing up tax dollars and should stop relying on public funding, and should come up with creative ways to seek private-sector funding, including fund-raising dinners. While this suggestion was treated with derision and did not account for much of the discourse, it is appropriate to ask, what is revealed by the particular approach taken by the three other candidates.

The last two decades has seen significant changes in the rhetoric surrounding cultural matters. We have moved a very long way from

Melina Mercouri's original proposal of European City of Culture, to the more recent and more commercial concept of 'Creative Cities', and *en passant* the concept of the 'creative class' has emerged in the discourse.

In 2010 the European Commission published a paper entitled 'unlocking the potential of cultural and creative industries'.

I believe it is instructive to consider the departure points of the Commission's Green Paper on this subject. The paper speaks of CCIs – or Creative and Cultural Industries. IT is fairly broad-ranging in that it does address several dimensions, but at its core, it remains embedded within a neo-liberal economic model.

The paper begins:

> In the recent decades the world has been moving at a faster pace. For Europe and other parts of the world the rapid roll-out of new technologies and increased globalisation has meant a striking shift away from traditional manufacturing towards services and innovation. Factory floors are progressively being replaced by creative communities whose raw material is their ability to imagine, create and innovate.
>
> In this new digital economy, immaterial value increasingly determines material value, as consumers are looking for new and enriching 'experiences'. The ability to create social experiences and networking is now a factor of competitiveness.
>
> If Europe wants to remain competitive in this changing global environment, it needs to put in place the right conditions for creativity and innovation to flourish in a new entrepreneurial culture. There is a lot of untapped potential in the cultural and creative industries to create growth and jobs. To do so, Europe must identify and invest in new sources of smart, sustainable

and inclusive growth drivers to take up the baton. Much of our future prosperity will depend on how we use our resources, knowledge and creative talent to spur innovation. Building on our rich and diverse cultures, Europe must pioneer new ways of creating value-added, but also of living together, sharing resources and enjoying diversity.

Europe's cultural and creative industries offer a real potential to respond to these challenges, thereby contributing to the Europe 2020 strategy and some of its flagship initiatives, such as the Innovation Union, the Digital Agenda, tackling climate change, the Agenda for New Skills and new jobs, and an industrial policy for the globalisation era.

As I said, many dimensions are addressed; however, at its core, the document is an attempt to shape European cultural policy to that which has been almost ephemeral in itself, the so-called Lisbon Strategy for 'growth and jobs'.

Please do not misunderstand me. Of course I am in favour of investment in creative and cultural industries, and jobs, and growth. Indeed, I believe that such investment produces a multiplier effect far greater than the investment itself. Where I take issue with the paper is in its localising of the value of creativity and culture to society in the jobs and growth that ensue.

When I was Minister for Culture during the period 1993 to 1997, I stressed the importance of the creative space and the immediately discernible contribution of the creative industries, be it film, music, or publishing, to economic wealth and employment. During that period, the value of the creative industries in employment terms was greater than that of the banking sector or the it sector. The multiplier was also greater, and had a greater regional effect. This situation has not changed, but I must warn that one could not assume that even in such an area there was an equality of participation. There was then, as there is now in Ireland, a clear divide based on class. The National Economic and Social Forum, in a study published in March 2007, gave statistics for December 2006 that showed clear differences:

> Those on higher incomes are three times more likely to attend classical concerts, and twice as likely to attend plays and art exhibitions, than those on lower incomes; this was also true in the use of public libraries.
>
> Even going to the cinema varies by class, with 69 percent of the middle class going to the cinema in 2007 compared to 42 percent of those from semi-skilled or unskilled backgrounds.
>
> People aged 35 to 44 had a lower attendance rate at a number of arts events, which may be related to family commitments in the rearing of children.
>
> A digital divide was also noticeable: 36 percent of the middle class downloaded arts-related material, compared to 21 percent of those from semi-skilled/unskilled backgrounds [. . .]
>
> Another striking statistic is that 40 percent of those using PCs in public libraries were non-nationals and 44 percent were unemployed.

These figures present a very serious challenge to a country with, until recently, a rich economy but with a social and cultural space that is seriously deficient in providing social protection and cultural inclusion.

Instead, the real value of creativity in society is to invent an agenda for living which defines the cultural space as wider than the economic space. Refusing to accept such a proposition is to seriously limit citizenship. The cultural space stretches in time back before any contemporary version of the economy. In that stretch, it raises all of the issues that are thrown up on what might be considered the ethics of memory. The cultural space should also include the various versions of the economy that are not yet born. The ethical issue posed is one of defending the integrity and freedom of that which can be imagined but which has not yet managed to be.

Culture, beyond all the definitional difficulties, is based on what we share. It is a process, one that is continually being reworked. In addition, because culture is shared, it constitutes the bedrock of the public world – a public world that is under threat from the demands of a destabilising privatised world, predicated on consumption, and the protection of a life-world often based on a fear of others. Thus, the shared trust of citizens in the public space is replaced by the insecurity of protecting private possessions.

To consider then the concept of the cultural space: the cultural space cannot be, I suggest, the residual of the marketplace. Rather, it is the space within which various forms of human activity are made possible. There is nothing abstract about this. The fact is that the cultural space, properly respected, can be not only a location for the arts but a source of vision, offering innovation in capacity for living, including the economic, and a necessary defining capacity for quality of life.

It is important to recognise the political implication of accepting the hegemony of the cultural space over the economic. A neo-liberal model that is over-reliant on market provision cannot produce such a space. Indeed, it tends to destroy it, colonising, as it were, the space of citizenship with the demands of consumption.

There is now a real need to emphasise that there is more than one version of an economic order. That which currently dominates in Europe is by no means the only one. Neither is it the most efficient or effective version of the connection between recovery and society.

Such an economy as currently prevails might be referred to as a 'depeopled economy'. What does this mean? What it means is that all is predicated on the needs and demands of the economic at the expense of all else. We do not work to live; rather, in too many examples we live to work.

Within such a model, so much else of our potential life experience is either denied us, or is seriously curtailed. In essence, issues pertaining to family, community and society are all too often superseded by an imposed devotion to maintaining the economy. But it goes much farther than that. Across the dimensions of space and time we are forced, be it in terms of enforced limitations in housing or, in the absence of public transport, to huge losses of social time to the demands of commuting to a work that is more often a necessity for economic survival rather than a choice for personal development. We must, I suggest, conclude that our current, over-determined model of the economy, and the economic space, is reductionist, clumsy and limiting.

Turning then to the discourse on cultural policy itself – there have been two major collaborations of an international kind that might have produced an international response to these issues: 'Our Creative Diversity' – the report of the World Commission on Culture and Development, published by UNESCO in 1995 – and the regional contribution from Europe entitled 'In from the Margins', published by the Council of Europe as its contribution to the debate.

Unfortunately, there has been little parliamentary response to these publications. While there were a number of valuable meetings in the preparatory phase of these works in different regions and countries, including Europe – ones that produced often valuable, thematic considerations, such as the Power of Culture Conference at The Hague, in 1996, which concentrated on the ethical basis of culture – the debate in the intellectual community has been deeply disappointing.

It is time for us to repeat that in debating and applying economic policies, there needs to be a critical engagement, with a critical relationship to, and a critical evaluation of, the society. There is a real need to engage critically with the world around us, particularly with regard to the way it is presented to us. In a globalised environment with a galloping concentration of ownership in the media, the dangers of an imposed homogeneity of consumption are real. I remain unconvinced as to the possibilities of local mediation of corporate globalising tendencies. The form may change but the rules and their impacts remain the same.

At the political level, the challenge is to identify democratic, participatory and empowering policies to ensure access to culture for the public at large and, through a better knowledge of other cultures, to encourage intercultural dialogue.

On a practical policy level, culture may be utilised to see to it that our past is 'harnessed' to our future, so as to ensure access and creativity, and sustain our cultural richness in its identities and diversities.

Culture can also prevent and treat some of the emerging tensions of our society. It can help build an understanding of the many facets of sustainability. It can bring about a new sense of solidarity. It can positively inspire the new economy, especially by acting as a means of empowerment and entitlement. It can be the bedrock from which we need to reach out to understand and respect other cultures with self-reliance. In other words, it is an ingredient of society and policy which needs to be brought in from the margins, because for many decades it has not received the attention it deserves from policy-makers.

Sadly today, across many parts of the world, culture is seen to be residual. It is marginal and tangential, and is in the worst instances abandoned.

I have previously argued, and did so as a government minister, as President of the European Council of Culture Ministers, that what are so sorely needed are meetings and seminars at which it might be possible to offer and discuss reservations of an ethical, political or social kind to the hegemonic discourse of neo-liberal market economics – the system which underpins the economic movements and engagements of our economic arrangements.

A decade and a half ago, I called for the recognition of the fact that if a cultural space were to be accepted even as at least equal, if not more important, than the economic space, then we would have had a space for a morally informed discourse. Unfortunately, we are currently in a period of a single, limited, intolerant, inhuman, discourse. That discourse for which I had called has not occurred.

It is surely now crucial, if not morally imperative, that we try to create such a space. What then might we do? Over a decade ago, it was suggested in the summary of 'In from the Margins':

1. Culture will have to be brought into the heart of public administration if it is to become more than what it is now – a partial and spasmodically effective instrument of policy.

2. Freedom of expression is a crucial principle, and cultural policies should establish a general framework within which individuals and institutions can work rather than intervene closely in what they do or say.

3. Europe's most valuable resource is its human capital. In many ways, this is not being exploited to its full – a failure which can be as damaging to economic prosperity as it is to the life of the imagination and the pursuit of happiness.

4. A more holistic approach to education is needed by transforming schools into culture-centred environments and enabling them to become foci of cultural life in their local communities.

5. It is time to restore the natural links between the arts and sciences, which were largely broken in the eighteenth and nineteenth centuries. Centres of technological innovation would help heal the long-standing schism in the industrial world between the so-called 'two cultures' of art and science. However, there is a danger that a dominant class will emerge, well-equipped and at ease with the new technologies, but consigning all those restricted by poverty and lack of training to the role of passive consumers, rather than full and active members of the communication society. This can be avoided only by a substantial technological investment in formal education and by the availability throughout adult life of retraining opportunities.

6. Cultural policy should foster unity while, at the same time, welcoming diversity. For good or ill, culture is a powerful promoter of identity. By emphasising one set of values against another, culture can be divisive and contribute to conflict rather than social harmony and mutual tolerance. It is essential that the development of arts and the conservation and exploitation of the heritage not only assert the commonality of European values but also reflect the multicultural variety which is characteristic both of Europe as a whole and of individual nation states.

7. The role of heritage in identity-building for Europe, nation states, and area-based and minority cultures needs to be acknowledged, and a new ethical approach is called for which recognises that the destruction of one community's heritage is a loss to Europe as a whole.

8. Culture has an important role to play, for it is the cement of the social and civic bond. An appropriate balance needs to be struck between the power of the state and, increasingly, multinational corporations and the freedom of the individual.

9. Governments should assist in the growth in the celebration of the 'local', which is a natural response to globalisation, and is often driven by the apparent cultural renaissance of image-conscious cities. The nurturing of creativity is essential if this is to be sustained: cities do not regenerate themselves spontaneously or at the behest of politicians.

10. The danger of Europe, and more particularly the European Union, closing in on itself should be avoided; culture can play a crucial role in this. National governments need to review their international cultural policies to reflect more adequately contemporary cultural practice and the changed political environment in Europe.

While quite conservative and even evasive on some of the more important issues, I do believe that 'In From the Margins' is better, and is in contrast to the European Commission's recent Green Paper. 'In from the Margins' remains a good starting point to redress the neglect of the cultural debate, and these points might be a good basis for what I hope will be a successful project: the recovery of the public world and the recognition of the importance of the cultural space.

It may be appropriate at this stage to say that whether or not one accepts the traditional role of the arts within a cultural policy, or subscribes to the new fashionable thinking, what is incontestable is that investment in creativity through the arts is of incalculable value. The heart of the debate, rather, is about how the potential of culture is to be treated in policy terms.

In recent times, the most frequently quoted source on the economic potential of the creative industries is the joint UNCTAD/UNDP 'Creative Economy Report 2008'. The figures given in this report are finding their way into economic proposals in a number of European countries. The most frequently used parts of the report are those which stress the contribution of the creative industries to growth, exports and employment.

'Creative industries' can be defined as the cycles of creation, production and distribution of goods and services that use creativity and intellectual capital as primary inputs. They comprise a set of knowledge-based activities that produce tangible goods and intangible intellectual or artistic services with creative content, economic value and market objectives. Creative industries constitute a vast and heterogeneous field dealing with the interplay of various creative activities ranging from traditional arts and crafts, publishing, music, and visual and performing arts to more technology-intensive and services-oriented groups of activities, such as film, television and radio broadcasting, new media and design. The creative sector has a flexible and modular market structure that ranges from independent artists and small-business enterprises at one extreme to some of the world's largest conglomerates on the other.

Today, creative industries are among the most dynamic sectors in world trade. Over the period 2000 to 2005, international trade in creative goods and services experienced an unprecedented average annual growth rate of 8.7 percent. The value of world exports of creative goods and services reached $424.4 billion in 2005, representing 3.4 percent of total world trade, according to UNCTAD.

Nowadays, in the most advanced countries, the creative industries are emerging as a strategic choice for reinvigorating economic growth, employment and social cohesion. The so-called 'creative cities' are proliferating in Europe and North America, revitalising the economy of urban centres through cultural and social developments offering jobs that are attractive, particularly to young people. The turnover of the European creative industries amounted to €654 billion in 2003, growing 12.3 percent faster than the overall economy of the European Union and employing over 5.6 million people.

Another important conclusion of the UNCTAD study is that developing-country exports of related creative goods (including computers, cameras, television sets, and broadcasting and audiovisual equipment) increased rapidly over the period 1996 to 2005 from $51 billion to $274 billion. This spectacular growth is indicative of the catching-up strategies being pursued in a number of developing countries to increase their capacities to supply value-added products to global markets. It also reaffirms the continually expanding demand for creative products that rely on these related industries for their distribution and consumption. This ever-increasing demand is further confirmation of the potential of the creative economy to contribute to economic growth.

One can easily see how, in responding to such possibilities, a certain excitement for the cultural industries emerges, even among those embedded in the most philistine version of the economy. Suddenly, there is money in all this culture!

Much more importantly than the volume of exports is the employment-creation capacity of the sector, and it is without doubt that the sector is unique, not only in its employment-creation potential, but in the sustainability of such employment, its capacity for regional dispersal, and the economically attested high multiplier it generates for local economies. Again, it is worth repeating that expenditure in this area is an investment that yields a short-, medium- and long-term value that is not paralleled in other, even the most modern, forms of the economy.

The challenge, however, is to use the discourse about the future of such activities in such a way as leaves us with an enhanced citizenship in general and a version of human activity that is fulfilling, liberating, and faithful to the power of the imagination.

I am reminded of what Patrick Mason, artistic director of the National Theatre Society in Dublin, wrote in his statement of policy in 2000:

> In the end, the National Theatre is not about making profit: it is about making theatre – theatre that is the most ambitious and rewarding that theatre can be. That type of theatre is not about social cachet, or glib marketing notions of 'Prestige' or 'Excellence', where real qualities are missing – qualities of depth, abundance, and intensity of vision. It is not about fashion, or this or that sociological agenda. It is about the enduring richness and integrity of its practice, about loyalty to the invisible world of the imagination and the spontaneous movement of the heart: above all, it is about staying true to the conviction of its founders, that all the people 'should have a more abundant and intense life'. Surely this latter objective – a more abundant and intense life for all the people – should be the aim, and economic policy the instrument that serves it.

I believe that it is achievable to create a bridge between the employment and material benefit of cultural practice and such issues of artistic integrity, and that we should strive to create such a bridge. It is not possible, however, to achieve such an accommodation without redefining the relationship between the economic space, the cultural space, and the citizenry. I have argued elsewhere that the cultural space is wider than the economic space – a fact that has been ignored consistently as we struggle to build even a debate on cultural policy within the European Union.

Recognising that the cultural space is wider than the economic space is of even more importance in times of high unemployment than in times of prosperity. The public spaces – libraries, schools, community spaces – are the spaces of all citizens, of all ages, whether in market-related employment or not.

A further issue that arises is whether provision for artistic activity within culture is accorded a central or a peripheral place in our planning.

A decade before I became Minister for Culture in 1993, in the heat of a debate about expenditure in the arts, in an article entitled 'The Case for the Arts', I wrote:

> The arts can be a fulfiling, expanding element of an entirely more fulfiled version of ourselves, and every penny invested in their encouragement and support today will be repaid tomorrow in all the individual and social benefits from more enhanced awareness and activity that includes elements of work, recreation and artistic activity.
>
> But it is not simply a matter of deferred gratification. The arts have benefits for us within our present society, not least indeed in enabling us to see beneath and beyond the taken-for-granted reality we call life. Bertolt Brecht's principle of the 'alienation effect', by which use is made as a source of audience interest of the tension between the play and life, is very relevant: the actor has a physical existence as a member of the audience's society, at the same time that he is in essence a member of a fictitious society. We can unmask our society, our relationships, our feelings through participation in the play as audience.

Those who paint for the first time, who dance, who act, will tell you of having felt that they had changed themselves in some way.

I believe very passionately that we have, by neglecting the integration of the arts into our mainstream experience, restricted ourselves to living at a fraction of our potential.

Unlike the characters in a play, we can change the script of our lives. We can reflect on the choice of selves, societies, masks and fictions. If we lock the arts away for an occasion, for an evening, for an indulgence, we lose out on much of their potential for the future, and for their revelatory and pleasurable potential now.

Let's have a policy then that goes beyond the squabbling for meagre crumbs and that sets valuable activities in competition for inadequate resources. A comprehensive policy is needed in all areas of the arts. Such a policy must begin by getting popular acceptance of the fundamental integral nature of artistic activity.

Acceptance of basic principles is not a philosophical preoccupation. The total state of the arts in Ireland reveals confusion rather than the diversity that is often claimed. Funding, it follows, should be commensurate with the importance such a view accords the arts.

Speaking now, almost three decades later, I am afraid that I am forced to make the same case. The absolute absurdity of cutting provision for spending in the cultural area repeats itself. Such spending is citizenship spending. Within the best policy, it has a powerful democratic dividend. Within the narrowest utilitarian version of the economy, it has a huge yield.

In crafting a cultural policy that would bring us into a new and fruitful area, it will be necessary to face up to the challenge of accepting that the existing neo-liberal economic paradigm is failing, with appalling, but knowable, consequences in terms of poverty, unemployment, and loss of social cohesion. Its assumptions, based as they were on the extreme individualism of such theorists as Friedrich von Hayek and Milton Friedman, have been proven to be not only wrong, but dangerous. The challenge to us all is to expose the assumptions of the paradigm that is destroying our prospects for the full realisation of our humanity.

A new form of political economy is slowly emerging. In South America, it is coming from the base, and is a little more respectful of culture and indigenous wisdom than any prevailing economic model. It is not without its problems, and its arrival in our discourse is not imminent, yet it is important as exemplar of the alternative world that is waiting to be born.

The strongest resistance to an emancipatory discourse is coming from the existing beneficiaries of an unequal society. Happy to reap the benefits from the cultural industries, they are not concerned that the world of entertainment has eschewed any responsibility for enlightenment or education, that it is characterised by monopoly in ownership, and by such a fragmentation in audiences as turns active citizens into passive consumers.

This form of economy, and its version of culture, represents a real challenge to us all. The choices are between inclusion and exclusion, activity and passivity, democratic control or monopoly, freedom and unfreedom.

Can economics be changed? I believe it can be changed. In a seminal paper, 'The Necessity of Utopia: Lessons from the Culture of Economics', Michael Volkerling in August 1999 addressed the contradiction that arose between changes, evident in the science of mind, that appear 'to have wholly rejected Cartesian dualism' in favour of theories of multiple intelligence and concepts of mind-body holism redolent of the Classical Age of Leisure 'on the one hand, and a set of cultural policy making practices on the other, that was only not influenced by the new consciousness but was happy to continue functioning within the failing and destructive model of neo-liberal economics. More than a decade later, this contradiction is not resolved, nor does it feature within the central discourse in economics or public policy.

Professor Volkerling took up this debate by contesting the 'fundamental proposition' of Australia's distinguished cultural economist, David Throsby, that economics and culture cannot be reconciled by virtue of their differing founding assumptions. Throsby had written that 'the economic impulse is individualistic and the cultural impulse is collective'.

The debate that was initiated has not been mirrored in the recent British or Irish discourse, yet the questions posed are of the greatest importance. We cannot avoid such fundamental questions as:

- Does the economy exist within a culture?
- Is culture separate from the economy?
- Is culture dependent on economic surplus?

Michael Volkerling reminded us that:

> What linked the ethical world of the individual with the State was not a common reliance on rational calculation, and the 'modern fact' such as characterises the prevailing economic paradigm. Instead the development of the 'full human capacity' of the individual was considered the best way of ensuring the emergence of the 'representative' citizen whose commonly shared interests it was the function of the state to safeguard. Such views substantially contradict the economic

conception of normative citizens as disaggregated, 'rational utility maximisers', devoted exclusively to their own self-interest.

Taking each of the terms in the title of my paper in turn – creativity, culture, citizenship and the economy – I believe that creativity is defined socially, and I reject an exclusive or elitist definition of creativity. Culture, I believe, has to be defined in a way that bridges the anthropological and artistic uses to which it is being put. Culture includes the riches of memory, and raises issues as to the ethics and politics of memory. Culture also is fluid rather than static, and the freedom of the imagination is one of its defining elements. Cultural policy has to respect these obligations. It can never be of the moment only, or be structured on short-term or narrow gains. Cultural policy too has to deal with the passage of time and inter-generational justice. It inherits obligations and creates a new legacy. The economy is best seen as instrumental within a society that has such a cultural policy.

Citizenship is, I believe, the test of both culture and the economy in terms of their end result. The economic has to be defined in such a way as to be of instrumental use for the achievement of democratic participation in an inclusive and sustainable way.

As Michael Vokerling sees it, the tasks are two-fold:

> First, it will require a reconnection of economic policy with its cultural roots to produce a rich, holistic discourse in which cultural knowledge is a necessary element and in which both economic and cultural priorities are reconciled. Second, it will call for a role for culture that links concepts of citizenship and community within a pluralist state operating in a globalised framework.

I sought to implement such a view, while I was Minister for Culture, and indeed at EU level when I attended the European Council of Culture Ministers. At European level, making progress in relation to cultural policy was very difficult. Direct references to culture do not appear in the founding treaties of the European Union. This is due to a number of reasons – and a feeling that culture had been abused in the past, that national identity was at stake, that the Council of Europe would handle the issue. Where it was recognised, in a minimal way, in the Maastricht Treaty, it did not enjoy parity with other dimensions of European life. In the UN Universal Declaration, culture also fared badly, and after decades of the subject being avoided, the issue of a right to culture resiled to a weak defence of heritage. The debate continues.

At home, all these suggestions have been contested, not only in recent times, but consistently over a long period. For example, during the period I was Minister, the *Sunday Independent*'s television correspondent of the day, Eilis O'Hanlon, wrote as follows of my policy on community arts. Having commented on a recent collection of poetry of mine, she went on to remark on my culture policy:

> Most nauseating of all, however, was the Minister's stated enthusiasm for 'community arts'. Everybody should have access to the arts, he insisted, and people should be encouraged to get in touch with their creativity. What he fails to appreciate, unfortunately, is that there are an awful lot of people who haven't got any creativity to get in touch with in the first place.

These views, published in 1993, came at a time when it was assumed that the wasteful argument between those who favoured

elitist versions of the arts and those who favoured the widest possible access, such as Dr Ciaran Benson (who had published a major
work in 1979 that I have no hesitation in saying, influenced all
my own policies while I was Minister for Arts, Culture and the
Gaelteacht). The reality is that excellence is achievable in the various
arts only through the expenditure of enormous effort, discipline and
courage. Those of us who supported community arts saw the social
cohesion that resulted, and respected the integrity of all forms of
the arts.

12.

The Role of the Public Representative in Today's Oireachtas

One of the least-noted portraits that hang on the walls of Leinster House is Orpen's portrait of Michael Davitt. I rarely see visiting groups pause in front of it, and indeed both the subject and the painter are without identification by way of a plaque or title. I became fascinated by the portrait in 1979 when the centenary of the Land War was being celebrated. Professor Theo Moody, Paul Bew and myself were amongst those invited to give papers at various venues in the west of Ireland. In the course of preparation of my own paper, I was intrigued by the transitions in Davitt's life, his journey from agitation and mass public meetings to parliamentary life, with its particular use of rhetoric, its committees and, of course, its limitations.

Davitt was not a member of Dáil Éireann, but his experience is interesting for comparative purposes. He was a member of the House of Commons after a period as leader of the most important late-nineteenth-century extra-parliamentary agitation: the Land War of 1879 to 1882.

He was thus somebody who straddled a divide — a divide some have seen as impossible to bridge — between public agitation and parliamentary language and ritual. Davitt, of course, also used parliament as a base for international issues, such as defence of the Jewish population and opposition to anti-Semitism. In his willingness to work within different systems and settings for change, he revealed a belief in the possibilities of each. His despair was reserved for those who lacked moral courage or who sought a non-emancipatory adjustment to the prevailing exploitation and its materialist base. The tenants would get the land, and what was left of the farm labourers after the Famine, and emigration, would be fed in the barn: that was the conclusion of not only Davitt, but of Land League colleagues such as Matt Harris.

During the time I have been passing that portrait, it has moved from one side of the corridor to the other. A smaller picture than any of the portraits from either the colonial period or later, it seems almost to have strayed in.

I sometimes reflect on the face in the picture. Is it anger? Is it despair? Is it lost faith that is caught in the brushstrokes, or is it, as is more likely, the indomitable rage of an idealist fated to see the rejection of the possibility of humane and emancipatory alternatives along the journey from secret society, through mass meetings, to the exchanges within parliament. No one of these stages need, however, be exclusive of any other. There are more than a few careers which demonstrate the combination of public agitation, public discourse, committee work and legislative reform.

What is clear from the portrait and, above all, from Davitt's life, however, is the importance of an authenticity of language which remains right through the ageing process. This is an authenticity based on moral and political conviction. The speech that is demanded on the side of a hill in Mayo must be drawn from the same well of moral conviction as the speech in Westminster on the rights of prisoners to be treated humanely in penitentiaries – prisons that shared a similar history to the factories, or the mills of Davitt's childhood.

Political rhetoric is important, and it is its loss that marks one of the fundamental changes from the founding period to what prevails in parliamentary practice of today. It happened to a certain extent in my own time. While I was a senator for the first time, between 1973 and 1977, there was no limit on time for second-stage speeches, and, while speeches were sometimes used for a filibustering purpose, such abuse was rare. The content is the test. One need no more than to take the debate on the Broadcasting Bill introduced in the 1970s by the then minister, the late Dr Conor Cruise O'Brien, and dissenting responses such as my own, and compare the speeches during that debate to current debates on the responsibilities and opportunities of public-service broadcasting, and draw one's own conclusion. It is not just that that passion has been replaced by a new emphasis on technical knowledge. It is that there is a decline in respect for the value, as source of political opinion, of political philosophy itself – which would produce a policy that might in turn be presented with a passion that was authentic.

In the early years, after my first election to the Dáil in 1981, the Dáil chamber witnessed powerful speeches from both Right and Left. The late John M. Kelly, for example, was an elegant, rational voice of a true conservatism for Fine Gael from 1973 to 1989. During that period, John Maurice Kelly and I almost needed each other as provocation, and the usual result was such a confrontation as was based on the clearly opposed assumptions of a class-based politics of Left and Right.

That style of political thought, practice and speech is long gone. Speeches in the Dáil are limited now by time. A twenty-minute slot may be divided among up to half a dozen deputies. Such an arrangement represents a convergence of interests – of the media, party whips, press offices, a market-driven print media at national level, a somewhat cynical media at radio and television level, and a public conceived of in terms of consumers within mass society, rather than citizens within a republic.

There is no such thing as a typical parliamentarian, either. Life as a parliamentarian inevitably involves moving between different worlds, the world of one's life experience, professional training or skill, ideological and political roots, the needs of constituents and the formal rituals, often archaic, of the parliamentary assembly itself. Many TDs will have been presocialised into these balances – but only to an extent – by their experience in local authorities dominated by a managerial system of control.

The balance between these worlds is, and has been, interpreted differently by different personalities over the years. Some have leaned toward the electoral base and concentrated on constituency work and have used a well-chosen silence, as much as public rhetoric, to facilitate their parliamentary survival. A smaller number of deputies again may have become absorbed by the rules, formal and informal, of the political system, some to the point that their communication is defined tightly by what is happening in the Dáil or Seanad. Some may go on to break their connection with public demonstration and agitation.

Politicians of the Left may differ from those on the right of the political spectrum insofar as their political recruitment differs. Those on the Left who arrive in parliament will usually have come through a recruitment process that will have involved agitation, public expressions of anger, or demand for political alternatives based on different assumptions of an economic or social-policy kind. Those on the right of the political spectrum will make the case for economic and social policy based on varying levels of market-driven ideology. They will rarely, if ever, describe themselves as being of the Right. What is market-driven is assumed to be what is natural: thus, they regard any state or indeed other regulatory alternatives as, at best, a necessary evil, or, more usually, a form of radical political deviance.

However, for most members, their political recruitment may have the common element of arrival through experience of local-authority service. This was true in my own case. While I was a university lecturer in political science and sociology, and had thus lectured on many other topics of the government of Ireland, I was elected to Dáil Éireann after seven years' local-government service, including its various committees.

As I write, I draw on not only that experience but on the fact that I have experience of most elective offices. I have been a member of the Oireachtas for over three decades. In 2010, I will have served nine years in Seanad Éireann and twenty-five years in Dáil Éireann. I was nominated to the Seanad in 1973 and served there until 1977. In that year, I failed to get elected by a margin of 2.24 votes. I was later to lose a Seanad election, in 1982, by less than a quarter of a vote – 0.024 of a vote. (Each Senate vote is valued at 1,000 for transfer purposes.)

Between 1977 and 1982, I was out of the Oireachtas, but became chairman of the Labour Party and active in local politics, having been elected to both Galway County Council and Galway City Council, including a period as Mayor of Galway.

I became a University Senator from 1982 to 1987. In that year I was elected for the first time to the Dáil for Labour as a TD for Galway West – a position to which I was re-elected at every general election since 1987. (In 2010 I announced to my constituents in Galway West, and to the Labour Party members, that I would not be standing again for the Dáil, since it was my intention to seek the Labour Party nomination for the Presidency of Ireland in 2011.)

While a member of the Dáil, I was given the privilege of introducing policy, a rare experience for many members with many years' experience. Between 1993 and 1997 I became a member of the Cabinet, serving as Minister for Arts, Culture and the Gaeltacht. In 1996, during the Irish Presidency of the European Union, I served as President of the Council of Broadcasting Ministers of the European Union.

To all this I did indeed bring my experience as an academic with a specialism in political science and sociology. The local-government experience helped too. Neither would be sufficient. There are significant differences between the senators' perception of their role and that of the Dáil deputies of theirs. Apart from that distinction, there simply is neither a typical senator nor a typical deputy, and both Houses of the Oireachtas are perhaps the richer for that. The balance between local and state interest, between the demands of representation and legislation, differ in terms of circumstances, constituency, age, and extra political expertise.

An underrated difference, I feel, is that between the urban Oireachtas member and his or her rural counterpart. The urban-based representative can go home at night – often, though, with the unenticing prospect of a constituency meeting or indeed a number of meetings. The rural representative usually spends Tuesday to Thursday in Leinster House, with finishing time of 9 o'clock approximately on Tuesday, and later sittings on Wednesday, and an adjournment at about 4 PM on Thursday. There is thus for rural representatives a period away from home each week.

Monday was normally reserved for local-authority meetings until the dual mandate was ended. Now it is reserved for work in the constituency office, for visits with constituents to Appeals hearings at local authority offices. Joint meetings, such as policing, which involve Oireachtas as well as local-authority members, are held on Mondays. Advocacy groups usually hold their meetings in the constituency on Fridays and over the weekend. Consultations in advice centres are scheduled in the period between Friday and Monday, inclusive.

More and more, in recent times, it has become necessary for rural representatives to travel to Dublin on Monday night. All special decision-making and strategic meetings of one's party, and executive or administrative issues, are discussed on Tuesday before the Dáil session starts, at 2.30 in the afternoon. Decisions on parliamentary issues, such as what topic will be selected for Private Members' Time, are usually made in this period. All the political parties have a parliamentary party meeting on either Tuesday or Wednesday. Labour, for example, usually holds its parliamentary meeting on Tuesday evening.

On Tuesday and Wednesday, on a rota basis, based on a number of deputies, opposition deputies have an hour and a half of debate on each evening for Private Members' business.

On each evening of a Dáil sitting, matters for the Adjournment are taken, with four Members selected. Each deputy chosen will have five minutes to make their case on the issue, and a Minister or Minister of State will have five minutes for a reply. The matter of an Adjournment motion is quite frequently sourced in the constituency of the deputy. It may also be a matter upon which there has been an insufficient reply to a Parliamentary Question.

Parliamentary Questions, Dáil Debates on legislation, Private Members' Times, and Adjournment Debates constitute the speaking opportunities for deputies. The speaking slots on main Bills are in scarce supply, and with the limits on time, backbenchers have a reasonable grievance that their speaking opportunities are very few. With the arrival of local radio, in addition to the local printed media, the anxiety of deputies to have a speaking slot, which would in turn generate a press release, has been considerably increased.

On their return to their constituency, deputies and senators will frequently have meetings of their parties or public meetings on local issues. Friday is a busy day in the constituency office, and Saturday, the usual day for advice centres – or 'clinics', as they are more usually called – may involve travel to outlying areas of the constituency as well as one's local bailiwick.

The need to combine constituency work with legislative work means that while in Leinster House, deputies will be in their offices for much of time, with the monitor switched on to Dáil proceedings in the main Chamber. Should there be a vote, the bells will ring for six minutes, and there are a few additional moments after it ceases, for the deputy to make it to his or her seat. In subsequent votes, the times are three and two minutes in each case. Electronic voting is now the norm: however, on budget votes, divisions take place through the lobbies. A whip of a party on a close vote may also call for a vote by other than electronic means.

As to the Dáil debates themselves, while the Cabinet members and frontbench spokespersons will use the greater amount of speaking time, and usually pre-circulate their speeches, the advent of electronic media has had some interesting consequences in terms of reporting the Dáil's proceedings. For example, in the old days, copy was filed by Dáil reporters even from midnight sessions. Now the tendency is to file on proceedings that precede six o'clock. On occasion, there is a media closure on coverage, after Leader's Questions in the later afternoon of Wednesday.

As to the general running of Leinster House, which houses both Dáil and Seanad and its staff: in recent years, an Oireachtas Commission has had the running of the Houses of Oireachtas devolved to it. Just recently, a media communications unit has been established with the purpose of explaining the working of parliament to the wider public, including schoolchildren.

Parliaments function in conditions of change. It is only reasonable that they respond to such change. What is needed, however, is a fully integrated package of proposals for change. How then might the parliamentary process be improved?

Irish politics is in need of reform; on that there is general agreement. In response to the loss of trust visited on the public by individuals and institutions political and financial, an adequate response is both urgent and unavoidable. There is, however, a real danger that by concentrating on the wrong part of the task of reform, the entire effort may end up as the feeding of a dangerous populism rather than achieving the changes that are necessary.

I believe we should not shrink from a fundamental reform of the legislative process itself. To achieve this, I repeat, it is important not to begin in the wrong place. A concentration on reform of the electoral process without, for example, examining the role and function of those who are elected to parliament by whatever elected system, those appointed to Cabinet or those holding senior positions in the public service, in terms of their legislative effectiveness and capacity, would be a futile exercise.

Recent decades have also seen the Dáil lose accountability to a plethora of extra-parliamentary bodies. As a consequence, there has been a serious erosion of transparency and accountability. For example, a Parliamentary Question to the Minister for Transport on a matter on roads or traffic impact in one's constituency may well not be answered in the Dáil on the basis that authority in this matter has been ceded to the National Roads Authority. Similarly, a question to the Minister for Health and Children on a health matter which is deemed to have been delegated to the Health Services Executive will be disallowed.

These are but some of the more serious and recent examples of

leaks from parliamentary accountability. While the agencies specified may indeed have a parliamentary section to answer parliamentary enquiries, the erosion of accountability is obvious. A
constitutional issue, indeed, arises as to what precisely the minister
involved in such a delegation must specify regarding what the
boundaries of policy and administrative matters are. In this area,
there is no clarity, and a serious question arises as a consequence as
to whether the responsibility of the minister to parliament, as
understood in the Constitution, has been eroded.

Any serious examination of the process of making, changing
and implementing legislation in Ireland would thus have to
acknowledge a serious case for reform of a general and fundamental
kind. Unfortunately, proposals for reform in recent times, drawn
from a recently recovered interest, have been aimed, almost exclusively, at simply where the populist dividend is highest – changing
the voting system – thus making the prospects for real reform far
less promising.

In my own evidence in 2010 to the Joint Oireachtas Committee
on the Constitution, which is currently addressing the issue of electoral reform, I suggested that the task of reform should begin by
addressing the monopoly of the right to initiate legislation enjoyed
by the Cabinet of the day. That monopoly has, I believe, had the
consequence of excluding many elected representatives from the legislative process. The weakening of a committee system, which is
already fairly powerless, and quite recent in many respects, is a further consequence. This weakness, and vulnerability to Cabinet
influence, as a result of a government majority on every committee
of a committee system too close to the government of the day, and
the administration it controls, has implications, inter alia, for the
appearance of expert advisors to government at such committees.
This is a problem that will develop.

One cannot but be aware of the recent developments in the United Kingdom surrounding the dismissal of Professor Nutt, a senior advisor to government whose professional comments were deemed unacceptable to the government he advised, and who was forced to resign by a government unwilling to allow the distinction between the professional scientific views he held and the views offered in satisfaction of his political advisory role. This is a problem that is certain to arise in the Irish case. The appearance of the Governor of the Central Bank before a Finance Committee of the Dáil could generate such a difficulty.

While proposals for reviewing our electoral system may have merit, then, the exclusive control exercised in relation to the right to initiate legislation is, to my mind, such a real obstacle to participation by elected representatives in making law, that it should have been given priority. This is where the task of analysis might more properly begin. Again, when it comes to making one's political contribution, or the building of a political career, unlike those systems where a person might concentrate on areas of interest or excellence, and make a career of such, advancement in political careers is confined, under the present system in Ireland, modelled as it is on the Westminster model, to membership of the Cabinet or the front bench.

The most impotent role of all, of course, in such a version of parliament, is that of the government backbencher. The contribution of backbenchers is undervalued in general and, while they may serve on committees, that service is circumscribed by the weak nature of the Irish committee system.

Were the monopoly of Cabinet in relation to initiation and serious amendment of legislation to be broken, were not just opposition spokespersons, but ordinary interested members of committees of the Oireachtas allowed to initiate, amend, or reject legislation, members of the Oireachtas could participate more meaningfully. In addition, those advocacy groups which attend committee meetings would have a real chance of influencing legislation at an early stage, where it counts. They, in turn, could put a far more meaningful advocacy to work in establishing a connection with citizens, which would, in turn, enable a more inclusive form of citizenship. Committees would have decision-forming, decision-shaping, decision-making and decision-taking functions available to them as a parliamentary capacity, rather than the current limitation of simply noting or responding to government policy, usually presented as a fait accompli.

What we have at the moment then is a weak, diffuse committee system that does not work in terms of connecting either citizens or groups to the parliamentary process. The newer, more recently created committees have both a government majority and an advisory system connected to the relevant Department.

Any comparative study would show that where a strong committee system is resourced and respected, legislators *may*, I emphasise, choose to build a career of service in a specific area, be it in health, housing, planning or other aspects of social, economic or cultural policy. While some legislator-representatives in such systems may well choose to move through a critical path of committees on their way to Cabinet or higher office, there is a meaningful legislative role for the many who may be interested. A comparison of the Scandinavian models of parliamentary committees with those of the Oireachtas would demonstrate this.

I am aware, of course, of the forensic achievements of the Public Accounts Committee on occasion, and its supporting staff. However, many of the other committees are add-ons, some created for reasons of political expediency rather than political transparency. The Foreign Affairs Committee, of which I am a long-standing member, came into being at the end of a fierce debate on the role of parliament in this area. In the Seanad debate I initiated in December 1981, when I proposed the terms of reference of a strong committee on foreign affairs, my proposals were resisted by a very articulate, but conservative, Fine Gael Foreign Minister, James Dooge. In his view, the government was charged with making and sustaining foreign policy. Parliament, at most, should strive for building a consensus on the government position. I, on the other hand, saw parliament as decisive in foreign policy, and I saw diplomacy as the professional craft for the achievement of policy ultimately sourced in parliament. A Foreign Affairs Committee, with limited powers, was established in 1993.

A legislation-producing committee system, at arm's-length distance from the Cabinet of the day, would also be more likely to garner such a level of media attention as might motivate the attention of political reporters, political correspondents, political editors and others. Thus, the public would not only have a committee system that worked, but one which was also reported, and was aimed at engaging in dialogue with citizens on the issues of the day.

This is an issue that has become all the more urgent as a result of the enhanced powers of national parliaments in relation to Europe that have been conferred by the passing of the Lisbon Treaty. National parliaments of member states have a role now that is much more than one of scrutiny. Parliaments have the right to initiate and amend legislation, and their relationship to the European Commission and the Council of Ministers is fundamentally changed. This means that parliament must now have such a committee system as can handle these new powers.

The concentration in recent discussion on reforming the electoral system, to the exclusion of other aspects of the legislative process, has been based on a renewed assertion that our existing electoral system produces clientelism. This analysis, however, is somewhat dated. It is also replete with assumptions based on the concept of political culture, which assumes sets of characteristics and political orientations held in common and presumed to have a determining effect. Political culture is a concept that has contributed little by way of understanding power and influence in Irish politics. Irish political science has, of course, with some rare and brave exceptions, avoided a class analysis of society. The flair for corporatist or neo-corporatist models has found greater favour and flourishes even today.

While studies of localism, personalism, or bailiwicks are interesting as descriptions of reputation strategies of management by TDs, that is the limit of their explanatory power. The older system of patronage and brokerage has been replaced by some systemic corruption sourced in the networks of a small, well-connected elite at the top of certain speculative sectors of the economy and banking system at one level, and by the mediation made necessary of an inflexible, ritualistic bureaucracy at the bottom at another level. At best, while the manipulation of local influence may affect intra-party competition, on the larger issues of power, or accountability, studies based on political culture tell us little.

For example, when I wrote of clientelism in the 1970s and of its effect on intra-party competition, it was clear that, while it did indeed continue to damage the state and its relationship with citizens, and it eroded the confidence of citizens, nevertheless it was changing. Later work would show that the survival of clientelist policies was mostly a form of response to an inflexible bureaucracy, and its function was one of reputation maintenance and enhancement for the representatives involved. I was aware, even then, that the greater threat to the state would come from the corruption to which I have referred, and from those networks of toxic influence in the surround of politics, which would go on to wreck our financial system and imperil our economy.

It had been known for decades that there was a shady intersection between the elective component of politics and a certain speculative activity in the economy, particularly in the property market for housing, and that this was easily identifiable. It was a feature of Irish politics that many knew this but chose to support, admire, or stay coyly silent about it. Irish politics also had, at times, its accommodating blindness in relation to the corrosive effect of single-party government on the administration of the state. Analysis of the corruption near the apex of this elite would have required an interest by political scientists in the state itself, in the distribution of power in Irish society, and in the networks of influence that leaned on the central state. Irish politics was, however, assumed to be non-ideological, Irish society classless.

While Basil Chubb's seminal essay of the early 1960s, 'Going About Persecuting Civil Servants', released a valuable discussion on the differing demands of the roles of legislators and representatives, insofar as it relied on the bland concept of political culture rather than an examination of the roots of corruption and inequality, and the processes of their reproduction, could only bring Irish political analysis to a certain point. Such work was, however, valuable, even seminal in its time, and while it has been succeeded in political science in Ireland by a concentration on voting studies, these latter have not demonstrated, it seems to me, anything of a fundamental value in theoretical terms as to the distribution of power or influence, or their consequences for representative democracy.

The reluctance in addressing the phenomenon of corruption in certain sectors of the Irish economy, and the jaundiced political connections that allowed it, or benefited from it, meant, of course, that its importance and implications in political and ideological terms were rarely stated. The fact that corruption was overwhelmingly a result of absence of regulation, supported by a politics of the Right, that it was rarely if ever a feature of the political practices of the Left, would never be stated. Phrases in the contemporary period, currently fashionable in the media, like 'the politicians' or 'the political class', are perceived by those who use them as safer, even if they are morally and intellectually evasive.

That the tribunals that were established in recent decades are still dealing with corruption is an indictment of such evasion. Again, the populist view, that we cannot afford such tribunals, is being covertly, and sometimes overtly, canvassed among the public by those with much to gain from the curtains being kept closed.

Clientelism is fairly empty of transmittable benefit and, while enhancing political reputations on a real or mythical basis, it is sustained more by a stubborn refusal to allocate the resources, establish the mechanisms, or hire the personnel that would strengthen citizenship, or address the shortcomings of a dehumanising bureaucracy. It is this icy world of bureaucracy, more than anything else, that sends the vulnerable in search of a sympathetic hearing. That hearing they frequently seek from their public representative.

In the commentaries on Irish politics, there are some basic features that get insufficient attention. At the root of Irish political analysis is an acceptance of anti-intellectualism. Irish politics has been analysed and discussed, even into the present period, with such an antipathy to philosophy, sociology and ideology that political commentary can be fairly accused of feeding an anti-intellectualism, and a cynicism which is deeply undermining of any belief among the public in the possibilities of politics itself, or the significance of political difference.

A fundamental change, not just in the legislative process, but also in the administrative system of government Departments, would yield a rich harvest. Those who work within the state know full well what a price has been paid for the absence of a serious critique of a system that is hierarchical, patriarchal, authoritarian, inflexible and, in relation to recent failures in regulation as to banking and the economy, unaccountable. Those who have to interface with this archaic and sometimes dysfunctional system turn to TDs as much for a sympathetic hearing as anything else. That is what happens every week in advice centres and in constituency offices.

While these encounters may be presented as tedious by some public representatives, they do keep public representatives informed on how the system is impacting on citizens. Listening to one's constituents can hardly impair one's legislative capacity. It is rather silly to suggest that public representatives make a simple vocational choice between the tasks of representation and those of legislation.

When I began in politics, such facilities as constituency offices, constituency secretaries, or Oireachtas Library Research Service did not exist. Deputies shared a room, and one secretary to seven or more members meant that a Dictaphone tape for members might be typed every fortnight or so. Today TDs have a parliamentary assistant and a constituency secretary. The facilities for providing a service to constituents, the preparation of material for meetings, research and media interviews, have been improved – or, quite simply, even made possible – by the provision of such services.

Not everyone sees it like this, of course, and some former members of the Oireachtas are inclined to suggest that a concentration on constituency service comes at the cost of legislative activity. However, the proof for this is not easily available.

Writing in the *Irish Times* in 2009, Dr Garret FitzGerald described the constituency office as 'hard to justify'. He suggested that TDs should get on with legislating. However, under the system of legislative monopoly we have, most TDs, as I have shown, are excluded from doing precisely that. Dr FitzGerald was silent on the consequences of the monopoly of the right of legislative initiation that is enjoyed by government – one that excludes many of these TDs. He left, and other analysts leave, the legislative monopoly intact. Changing the voting systems, while leaving the role of politician unexamined, seems to me to be no more than the pursuit of a cosmetic change, which, while it might satisfy populist demand at a time of damaged political trust, does not address the real tasks of the political change we do indeed need. Those politicians who are pushing to gain the populist accolade are not in the vanguard when it comes to more fundamental change.

None of the foregoing is to say that examining the consequences of the electoral system is not important; rather, it is to say that it has its value only as part of a more general critique of the legislative process.

I believe, further, that any political scientist serious about reform must question the origin and consequences of the hegemony of the Department of Finance in relation to other departments of state. I believe that such hegemony does not have any clear constitutional base. It is simply a relic of Westminster practice, invented for very different times; that it was simply a mimicry of Treasury practice in its origins and is today a dysfunctional arrangement in administrative terms.

If, as an alternative to such a hegemony in Cabinet practice and Department of Finance final approval for all capital and current expenditure, Cabinet allocated blocks of capital and current expenditure to significant areas that had been chosen on a transparent policy basis, and then made them accountable to committees with real power, one could see how such an enhanced political ability to respond to change could be achieved, with benefit to members and, above all, to citizens in general.

It is important to address some of these crucial issues of governance, transparency and legislative efficiency, before one decides to accept the extreme populism and dangerous anti-democratic myth that there is too much representation; that the number of representatives should be lessened, should be chosen in a different way, or have their facilities for interaction with their constituents reduced, or even abolished.

Finally, an important issue, one that I must stress, is that parliamentary representation and legislation is but one part of the task of political change. The raising of issues, the development of moral and political alternatives, and respect for political consciousness, political education and public agitation are not made redundant by pursuit of parliamentary representation. Rather, such dimensions of political life are intertwined and, while the role of parliaments may change, the alternative, of sweeping away such mediating institutions as parliament, of pursuing a naked conflict, is unlikely to achieve fundamental change, such as the expansion and deepening of democracy at all levels and in all institutions.

Another view that has become popular in disconnected academic writing as well as in sections of advocacy is that of opting for such a radical communitarianism as would constitute starting all over again. I choose to see this as rather similar to an invitation to a discourse on lifeboat management before a decision has been made to abandon ship, or a conclusion reached that the ship is sinking. What is also clear to me is that such discourses need not be exclusive of each other as part of a general non-sectarian reflection.

We need reform. To achieve it, we need such a discourse as can draw on our own and others' genius for creativity. The current debate has, depressingly, begun in the wrong place. The achievement of the most vocal, but not necessarily the most thoughtful, of critics, may well be one of securing a place at the front of the righteously enraged crowd whose trust has been squandered, but it may be at the cost of genuine legislative reform or deepened citizenship. Should that continue, it would deliver a dark future. The prospects are not good. For myself, it is a privilege to serve, and while it would have been a joy to have been passed out by radical reforming parliamentarians anxious to compete in the task of developing and extending democracy, that was not to be.

The role of public intellectuals – or a variant thereof, intellectuals in politics – is coming to the fore again in recent debate. Irish politics, however, has been perceived as having an antipathy to such aspirants. Indeed, a former taoiseach, Bertie Ahern, has written in his recent memoirs that he did not have much time for them as colleagues.

What he was referring to in particular was a group of Labour TDs. During the 1960s, a number of intellectually qualified people became active in politics – particularly in the Labour Party. Their first contest was the general election of 1969, which, while it gave Labour its highest ever number of votes, did not give the party a sufficient number of seats to sweep away the old political structures, as Labour had sought in its 1969 manifesto that year – a manifesto enthusiastically, and courageously, supported by its membership, including the intellectuals for whom Mr Ahern recalls an antipathy.

Indeed, one may well ask if it is acknowledged anywhere in our media or in academia that there is a need, even a space, for public intellectuals in Irish politics. There certainly is a need for the participation of those privileged enough to have an opportunity for education, professional training and reflection, to cross the bridge to the public world. It is surely nonsense to suggest that thought and practice contradict each other. The truth is, however, that the tacit and overt forces of conservatism in the institutions are not amenable to change in a single Dáil term. Many of the most reforming minds have simply not survived long enough electorally to see the changes they sought advanced. Others have wearily retired from the fray. Some have been comprehensively rejected by the electorate.

As a witness to the contribution of these deputies of 1969, I can say that the view that there is no space for such intellectuals in Irish politics is entirely false. Such a view is not supported by the Dáil record or by their work. They were in continual confrontation with a bureaucracy that had accommodated itself to what was virtually single-party rule. In addition, it is important to note that there was, as a result of their participation, probably at no other time as good a connection between the passion of public debate and parliamentary rhetoric. The speeches given in the Dáil had the ring of authenticity to them. It is a very false revisionism that presents, in retrospect, any summary of such careers in terms of a collision between political idealism and the so-called realism of political decision-making.

The public in Ireland of course relies on the media for its information, and often sole or slight knowledge of politics and politicians. How then is Irish political practice presented and discussed? One of the features of the contemporary discourse is its concentration, in terms of time, in shrunken context in the absence of historical perspective. The shallowness of the narrative that constitutes political discourse is justified by an appeal to the diminished concentration time it is suggested can be assumed for an Irish public regarded, even by its public-service broadcaster, as consumers rather than citizens.

In terms of time, and in the absence of a serious intellectual engagement, the development of a culture of celebrity has come to dominate in recent times. This has emerged through a curious intersection of, and collaboration by, personalities drawn from the ranks of politicians, commentators and editors. It is enormously facilitated by the technology of a visual media that stresses sound-bites and set-pieces rather than any elucidation of policy. Indeed, political discussion can reach such an absurd point as to find political analysts interviewing each other. Within the parliamentary discourse itself, such a sense of immediacy comes to dominate. The politics of the day becomes simply a reaction to the headlines of the day. The ensuing discussion then, in turn, guarantees a headline for the following day.

Another feature of the contemporary political discourse is an uncritical acceptance of expert opinion in areas such as the economy and social policy. While much of such commentary is of course valuable, a significant proportion of the opinions are contestable. Any views that might be emancipatory in the best sense are usually disallowed on the basis that they are potentially ideological and, in any event, would require more than a couple of minutes to elaborate. It is hard to disagree with the opinion that there is in recent times a significant 'dumbing down' of political commentary, justified usually on the somewhat false assumption that the public would not understand. This fits with that more general tendency in the society to replace the demands of citizenship with those of consumers, to which I have referred already.

The structure of the production arrangements of some of our current-affairs programmes are quite revelatory in this regard. The expert participation which will be presented as neutral, as dealing with the indisputable facts, is usually facilitated in the first segment. The second, discussion segment, is then presented with political representatives and others offered as discussants, who would not understand the intricacy or complexity of what preceded. The recently briefed anchor or presenter then serves as a kind of echo of the expert opinion of the first segment, and, of course, it may end with: 'That, I am afraid, is all we have time for.' Indeed, the issue is not the team; it is the concept of public broadcasting that is at stake. In a mixed competitive model of broadcasting, the battle for viewers adjusts itself to the market. A public that views itself as disaggregated consumers, rather than citizens, gets the broadcasting that consumers want. Society at large, and future generations, may be the loser, but this is not accorded a central importance, in an atmosphere where public-service broadcasting has declined or even departed.

Many Irish politicians are reluctant to offer criticism of the media in general or, in particular, of the more than twenty-five members who observe proceedings from the press gallery for part of the week. Thursday and Friday are used by many such eminent commentators for the purpose of sharing information and gossip for their columns in the following Sunday's papers. Thus, a voyeuristic interest in personal details is frequently offered as a substitute for the political proceedings of the preceding week. While newspaper sales may have a minimum requirement of titillation, it is surely regrettable if this leads to the near-total exclusion of such material as could have been the basis of political reflection or indeed public education. Some political editors have been known to harass their staff to the point where these reporters have become desperate for a story and have confided their distress to politicians.

In general, in the Irish media, there has been a decline in the historically or theoretically informed long piece. The absence of an essay tradition in the Irish print media – with significant exceptions, such as Fintan O'Toole, Vincent Browne, and some others – is notable, and has had the consequence of a reliance in the political pages by way of substitute on political gossip, or loose speculation as to the formation of government – this latter in personalised terms rather than policy terms. Thus a contemporary Irish anti-intellectualism and a false historical revisionism combine to sustain what should not be sustainable.

Given the transient nature of their existence, parliamentarians themselves are inclined to fit themselves, and their practices, seamlessly into a system that they have after all waited a long period to enter, and, in the case of some, a system of which they are in awe.

Among the most serious influences that threaten the parliamentary system at the present time, is the tendency of parliamentarians and their parties to capitulate to a populism that is rooted in the disappointment of consumers — consumers whose expectations were cultivated in a highly individualised society, rather than in any concept of responsible and inclusive citizenship. Indeed, recent changes in the Houses of the Oireachtas themselves reveal the influence of this culture; they speak of consumer satisfaction rather than adequacy in citizenship terms. Thus any deep commitment to the extension of democracy in a representative sense, or in the sense of such institutional reform so as to facilitate an enhanced public participation, is put on the back-burner.

The capitulation, too, of public representatives to a populism based on cynicism is reflected in the rush by some of the more publicity-hungry representatives to endorse a reduction in the number of deputies, the abolition of the second chamber, and a change to the electoral system. The last is based on a rush to provide an acceptable response to the demand for change, and thus its aim is the achievement of populist satisfaction at any cost, rather than on the implementation of the results of any detailed analysis of the functional possibilities of our existing legislative process or its reform.

Quite worryingly, too, academic work on politics seems set to disappoint. Long-out-of-date work is invoked out of context in justification of the case for changing our electoral system. This includes, as I have said, my own work on clientelism, written nearly forty years ago. Whatever change is proposed to the electoral system should, I believe, be based on adequate empirical research – research that has been made available for public discussion and consideration, and which takes account of what is available through comparative research. I understand that this is happening in the recent research being conducted for the committee on the Constitution, and I welcome it.

Writing in celebration of fifty years of the Dáil, the late Basil Chubb entitled his summary piece for RTÉ 'Ireland: A Successful Democracy'. He based his evaluation on the achievement of continuity and stability, and was aware of the benefit to the Irish parliamentary system of a familiarity with the Westminster model. He noted a successful adaptation, in the Irish case – better than many other post-colonial experiences.

There is, of course, an advantage to institutional systems having models upon which to base their practice. Few could doubt, for example, that the presence of a great competitor in the BBC was both a challenge and an aspirational standard to Irish public-service broadcasting. The Reith principles, though admittedly paternalistic, gave an authentic commitment to the functions of public-service broadcasting when it defined the purpose of broadcasting as a vocation and a duty to inform, educate and entertain. These were mostly emulated, and they guided the early days of Irish broadcasting.

Similarly, basing one's parliamentary arrangements on the Westminster practice had its undoubted advantages of continuity and stability, but it has had some more serious disadvantages. Archaic practices, and the domination of ritual over reasonable change, have at times been a serious obstacle.

What is needed now is fundamental reform to give us an appropriate legislative process for an inclusive republic, one that is amenable to change in contemporary conditions. An invigorated parliament, with engaged representatives, confident and open about their differences, including their ideological differences, must be part of that. Any lesser form of change will serve us badly. The era of parliament is not over, but it needs urgent renewal. I return to Orpen's portrait of Davitt. The intensity in the face shows none of that settled composure cynicism displays. Rather, there is an angry determination to go on.

Cynicism has the capacity to destroy our democracy. We do need real change, and we can have it, if it becomes a popular political demand, and even if that is not the achievement of this generation, it may be the project and achievement of a future generation that possesses a greater conviction.

13.

The Concept of the Irish Peasantry:
A Reflection

Being asked to give an opening address to the Thirteenth Lady Gregory Autumn Gathering, an Annual Gathering at Coole Park, carries quite a challenge. I am aware of the significance of their reflections and the writings that emanated from the house and setting at Coole Park. It is important at the outset to make what I feel to be an important clarification. Coole, and its district, is a place, the rich experience of which, with its valuable folk inheritance, was the source for the early tasks undertaken by Augusta Gregory. Her work, however, in terms of making a record of what has been lost, is only part of her achievement. It was the first stage of a long journey that led to partnership in creating a suggestion as to what might have been, in imaginative terms, a symbolic structure for a life-world shared by what had come to be regarded as the Irish peasantry.

Before I say a little more about this concept, however, I would like to reflect on the significance of Coole Park itself. The name has a symbolic significance that goes beyond a simple sense of place. The symbolic layers are many. The use of the term 'Park' itself indicates an attempt at an intention to create, or perhaps make a statement as to the importance of, order.

The term 'Park', too, has an unmistakable connotation of something created by human effort that seeks to harness, engage or transcend the purely natural. The creation of order in the midst of chaos, or of order threatened by the disruption of chaos, is a theme that I believe is quite constant in Anglo-Irish literature. I believe, for example, that it is possible to read the arrival of Christy Mahon into the world of Pegeen Mike in John Millington Synge's *The Playboy of the Western World* in such a way.

Neither space nor time allows further unravelling of the intention that may be behind the making of a park. Was it a perceived oasis in a chaotic surround, a defiant gesture of resistance to the dispossessed, or with its enclosing walls a deterrent to those who might encroach? For my purposes this evening, I feel it is important to stress the significance of Coole Park as a term. I use it to recognise the significance in an ideological sense of the term 'park'. In heritage terms, Coole Park is significant, obviously for its house, demolished in 1941, but also for what was planted, and the purposes for which the grounds were laid out. Might I suggest, further, that replacing 'Coole Park' with 'Coole' is a serious mistake on the part of the Office of Public Works or other such state bodies. So much is missed by such a substitution.

Seamus Heaney, in a seminal essay on heritage for the Royal Institute of Agriculture's 150th-anniversary year, captured the importance of Coole Park not just as space but as symbol, describing it as:

> this large enclosed space, surrounded by the woods and lakes of Coole Demesne disposed at different levels, traversed by walks artfully planted with trees and shrubs. This area is not uniquely an Irish phenomenon. This garden is an image of the achieved life of civilisation. Mythically it is endorsed by the story of Eden,

where within the charmed enclosure of the garden, harmony and fulfilment and a radiant consonance between desire and reality were constantly afforded to human inhabitants. Outside was the unformed, the inchoate, the unspeakable, the unknown. Inside was the defined, the illuminated, the elect, the fully empowered human life, and even when the story proceeds to its greatest crisis, and man and woman have been cast out into a thorn-world of sweat and tears, the garden remains as a dream of a possible redeemed life. It becomes a social and architectural form.

Reading such from Seamus Heaney, the removal of 'Park' from the signage to our heritage is of some significance, and perhaps, not unrelated to the passing or ignorance that sought and achieved the demolition of the house in 1941, it reflects an early form of the vandalism that has its successors in present times in such acts as putting the impatience of the National Roads Authority over the nation's heritage in terms of policy.

A lesson perhaps we have not learned is the importance of thinking in inter-generational terms. The price we pay for this, our obduracy, of course, is that of visiting the consequences of ignorant and short-term thinking on future generations.

Heaney's reflection was on the passage of buildings from a utilitarian purpose to, over time, a symbolic existence. His essay in 1989 took account of the co-existence and tension between what was esteemed to be high, and what is now given recognition as vernacular culture.

I would like to make a further reflection, beyond issues of heritage, on the concept of peasantry itself. I believe it to be a concept of limited utility in anthropology, without sufficient precision of definition in sociology but, perhaps, useful, as a source of controversy, in literature and history.

The outstanding critique of pseudo-pastoral and the romanticising of the peasantry is that of Raymond Williams, particularly in the second chapter of his *City and Country*. The invention of an artificial rural idyll has been quite a feature of the reaction to the city as part of a comprehensive anti-urbanism that we can detect in the writing on British society in the nineteenth century. We had, however, our own extended flirtation with the invention of a bucolic peasantry. Antoinette Quinn's biography of Patrick Kavanagh refers to that period when, encouraged by Leslie Daiken, Kavanagh wrote as 'the representative of those Clay-faced sucklers of spade-handles'.

The experience and insights of Kavanagh were such as to effortlessly debunk the generalisations and over-simplifications of those who had an invented version of purity, simplicity and indeed heroism of country life. These last two words indeed themselves contain a contradiction. There never was a simple singular version of rural life, no more than there is a simple singular existence as an inhabitant of Dublin or Galway today.

Rural Ireland was layered into different classes, moving from extreme vulnerability, where only the sale of one's labour was a source of life, right through potato-plot access, opportunity to graze a cow, up through the allowed privilege system of land agents and landlords. The notion of a homogeneous Irish peasantry is a myth, and a seriously distorting myth at that.

Irish society was divided in terms of levels of precarious dependency on land for the production of food before the Famine and after the Famine; and indeed those who emigrated were overwhelmingly drawn from what was left of the agricultural labourers and the lower echelons of tenants-at-risk.

While the Land War of 1879 to 1882 was fuelled by the desire for even an elementary security, it too was succeeded by the emergence of even deeper class divisions: a predatory class who would come to exploit their own people with a ruthlessness as vicious as that of any absentee landlord. The grazier class which emerged, often in co-operation with a section of the shopkeepers in the towns, came to own vast tracts of land, often as great as the estates which they had replaced.

The difference between them and what preceded them, being that a shared religion, the sending of a son to Maynooth, or the provision of a dowry for a daughter called to the convent provided a set of masks to cover the native predators' actions.

The gatherings that took place in Coole Park, that gave us so much of the Anglo-Irish Literary Revival, were not happening in a conflict-free society. 'The peasantry', as a literary construct, might be perceived to be at peace with a long folk memory, but those on whom such a construction was being attributed, contemporary accounts show us, were by no means at peace.

Beyond their differing prospects for survival, life or emigration, what did the neighbours of those who gathered at Coole Park share. What did they have in common? Were they the carriers of an irrepressible memory of what constituted their shared heroic history? Was the defining characteristic of this rural people that they were carriers of myth and all the rich resources of the heroic? Perhaps.

I believe that it is not easy to conclude that that which was gathered by Augusta Gregory constituted an archive of unbroken and seamless inheritance. What if that which was available constituted the broken shards of a previous world, and one recorded in a different language to that which would be used to deliver an imaginative agenda of myth and poetic resonance from those anxious to equip a new and independent state with appropriate tools for tilling the fields that constituted the politics of memory?

At the time of Augusta Gregory's first gatherings, it is plausible that a new language, with old rhythms, was emerging, just as in another place in the seventeenth century, in the Caribbean, the slaves adjusted their African rhythms to the movements of the formal dance they viewed through the windows of the Plantation House; or then again, perhaps it was that after the initial project of collection, important as it was, a later project emerged out of Coole Park. One that had, as its aim, the establishment, and the acceptance, of what the heroic might appropriately be for an Irish people in new conditions.

There is in Yeats' project something of the character of such an imposition. I speculate as to whether what began as a voyage of discovery by Augusta Gregory evolved into a project complete with ritual that was splendid, rich and enabling, but in little sense organic. This is not to take from the endeavour, nor to diminish the achievement, but it suggests that the artifice of park, the civilising thrust of garden, rather than the discovery of a universal strain of imagination, that we might call the essential symbolic life of the Irish peasantry, was the fruit of the project.

James C. Scott, in his work, has also provided us with a further corrective as to views of the peasantry. He has shown us that theirs is not a single discourse, nor can their demeanour be accurately judged to be one of submission. They have available to them the tools of irony and language, which can be adjusted to the upstairs or downstairs of their lives.

While the hidden transcripts of their lives may not constitute the formal history of a period, it involves the construction and use of a transcript as rich, humanist, essential and complex as the formal one. Such a transcript is both a defence and an art-form in its own way.

There has not been a homogeneous population in rural Clare or

Galway for generations. That said, is it not fair to say that it is, perhaps, in the non-verbal, in the music that has come down in a relatively unbroken tradition, or in the long echo of unaccompanied singing, that we can best access, and encounter, what was once shared in common.

The projects that flowed from Coole Park are not lesser because they were derived from or connected directly with myths inherited. They, I feel, should be judged on their own terms as cultural contributions in times of contradiction.

Finally, looked at now, three-quarters of a century later, the arguments of the 1930s as to what constituted a peasant, with their competing stereotypes, seem little less than a set of tools for inclusion or exclusion in literary circles and publications. Such stereotypes visited serious consequences on artists, and for many, it would seriously distort their work and undermine their confidence. For example, for some, Patrick Kavanagh was moving too far from the plough. As Antoinette Quinn puts it: 'It seemed to the bemused Kavanagh that everyone was trying to climb on the peasant bandwagon.' Everyone was writing in a rougher, and what was perceived to be a more rural and peasant, way. Quinn tells us that 'The Plougher' of Padraic Colum was taken as a standard, and as she puts it:

> To sustain his role as peasant-poet, Kavanagh only needed to make the occasional reference to trees, birds, weather, seeds or soil in his verse; no display of more specific agricultural imagery was expected.

Meanwhile, other writers were dislodged in their confidence as to the value of their own work, regularly testing themselves against the standard of what a polite London readership required in its literature by way of peasant portrayal. This is a conversation that Liam O'Flaherty, for example, regularly held with himself, and it features in his letters to his patron and friends.

Free of the harness of distortion, Irish writers since, such as John McGahern, have accessed universal aspects of the human condition without sacrificing either place, intimacies, or the competing realities of the century and circumstances in which they lived. For them, the concept of the Irish peasantry would have appeared reductionist, limiting and not particularly useful. Perhaps, then, it is time to see the concept as not having an empirical significance, but something useful for a time, and delightful, even valuable, in the artifice it enabled.

Address to the Thirteenth Lady Gregory Autumn Gathering,
Coole Park, Gort, County Galway,
September 2007

14.

Sugar, Tribes,
Dispossession and Slavery:
Montserrat and its Irish Connection

I first heard of the Irish connection with the island of Montserrat in the mid-sixties. John C. Messenger and his wife Betty gave some presentations in Dublin on what they termed 'the Black Irish' of Montserrat, and the discussion which ensued on habits, food and speeches reached Galway, where I was a student. I was later to meet the Messengers at Indiana University in Bloomington in the following year, and I had become familiar with their work and the work of Aubrey Gwynn, to which they referred.

However, it was to be many years later, almost two decades in fact, before I encountered again the theme of the Irish connection with the Caribbean. In the eighties, in Galway and elsewhere, a fashionable tendency had emerged of identifying with the Tribes of Galway as examples of some kind of Medici-style greatness. I had a jaundiced view of this. We were in Ireland at the time going through a period of such extreme revisionism that descendants of tenants were inclined to project themselves backwards in history to being occupants of the Big Houses, where, of course, in reality but a favoured few of their ancestors had, with a harshly required deference, laboured in the kitchens or bent their backs in the gardens. It was as if the pretensions and illusions of the present required a revision of the past. This atmosphere influenced the consideration of the Tribes of Galway and their place in the history of the city.

I had at this time been working on a sociological paradigm of Irish emigration, and while looking for early work on Irish voluntary and involuntary migrations came across the more detailed work of Reverend Aubrey Gwynn SJ on the Irish in the Caribbean and South America. There they were, the Blakes, Lynches, Kirwans, Bodkins, Skerretts – five of the fourteen Tribes of Galway – to be known later as adventurers, the euphemistic title given to those who sought to ruthlessly exploit new territories for the satisfaction of the ruling and newly fashionable European addictions of nicotine and sugar. It was a side of the Tribes of Galway not usually given attention.

Faced with expropriation of their property, exclusion from governance, commercial practice or indeed meaningful participation in society – exclusions made on the basis of a clear religious discrimination – many propertied Irish, both Old Irish and Anglo-Irish, looked to their network of trade contacts abroad for survival, and prospects of a new fortune. Thus, for example, second sons, from such families as that of the Mayor of Galway, the Blakes, would have a second son seeking his fortune in the Caribbean, with the intention of returning home and living in the style to which they felt they were entitled. It would be easy to suggest that thus, at least in some cases, the victims of colonisation became in time the colonisers in a new setting. But that, as we will see, would be an over-simplification.

We in Ireland are much more familiar with a historiography that stresses the forced migration of our people, our experience as victims. In the case of the Caribbean, Cromwell's forced transportations of the populations of Drogheda or Galway are areas that come most easily to mind as the stuff of school history lessons. While a revision has been useful, its excesses in turn have served to diminish the cruelty of imposed exile and the poisonous ideology of empire that drove it.

The Irish who found themselves in the Caribbean in the seventeenth century, then, were not similar in background or motivation. Neither were the social settings from which they left in any sense homogeneous. The Irish connection with the Caribbean in general, and Montserrat in particular, is multi-layered in source and consequence.

While the early Irish settlements in South America to which Aubrey Gwynn refers, such as the Amazon settlements of the Purcell brothers, as early as 1626, may have an exotic quality, they are not typical. By the time the main Irish arrivals in the Caribbean happen, the Irish have had the experience of their own country being plunged into one of the most conscious and ruthless re-settlements in history. A full half-century after the defeat of the Irish by the English forces at Kinsale in 1603, the Irish were going through the beginning of the end of the Gaelic Order – which was far from being an ideal society, I hasten to add. Yet the colonisation which would now be unleashed had a profile that was brutal in these new settings and was clearly racist. The colonisers' rationalisation in general has a package of assumptions as to the superiority of the coloniser and the inferiority of the colonised, be it in terms of the experience of childbirth, the expression of grief, forms of economy, patterns of agriculture, or animal husbandry.

There were about 15,000 settlers in Munster by 1622. Indeed, Quinn estimates that about 150,000 settlers entered Ireland between 1586 and 1700. The population increased from less than 1.5 million people to over 2 million by 1641. This settlement was achieved by measures that included dispossession and forced exile.

It is possible to envisage a situation then where, in addition to the consequences of the Cromwellian vengeance, some surviving Old Irish, and many Old English, lost land. Their experience was one of being forcibly relocated or left with no option other than having to choose relocation. They in turn pushed others to even more inhospitable land. Into the population-congested poorest area of Connacht came even those not only more destitute, but carrying with them a new experience of dispossession which would in time enter the culture as a dominant theme of collective memory. It would also be, in cultural terms, the beginning of a great loss of dignity and security.

On the other side of the world, the Caribbean in this period, between 1630 and 1700, was receiving almost two out of three of all emigrants from the British Isles. More than half of these were indentured servants.

The Irish in the Caribbean included masters, migrants from Virginia, indentured servants, conscripts, and those families and individuals who had been deported from the ranks of those who had lost in the Cromwellian sieges.

There is a need to draw a distinction then between some quite qualitatively different types of Irish who arrived in the Caribbean in the seventeenth century. For example, there were categories that included:

- The adventurer speculative Irish, such as the Blakes, Lynches, Kirwans, Trants

- The indentured servants with some semblance of choice in the early seventeenth century
- The forced indentured labourers with little or no choice, particularly in the second half of the seventeenth century
- Those transported from institutional settings, be it a bridewell or an orphanage, as an insatiable demand for labour came from the speculative economies of tobacco and sugar
- Those families and individuals transported as a result of the Cromwellian conquests

What then was the relationship between the dispossessed or exiled Irish abroad in a new setting to the economics of empire, colonisation, and in time slavery?

It is a story the full texture of which is difficult to recover; for example, I believe that it is near impossible to discover the life of the indentured servants. While it may be accurate to see all Irish as complicit in the perpetuation of further layers of exploitation and cruelty on black slaves, I believe that there is no one simple Hibernicist story, no more than there is one simple Africanist story that stands in competition with it. A recent writer, Donald Harman Akenson, appears to assume in his book *If the Irish Ran the World: Montserrat, 1630-1730* that the Irish were not only a statistical majority among whites at the beginning of the eighteenth century, but also that they were a homogeneous entity. He goes on to suggest that Irishness can carry its own tendency to the abuses associated with imperialism. He works back from this brief early-seventeenth-century window of experience to make some generalisations about Irishness in general.

Montserratians should not be asked to choose between such reductionist simplifications. For example, the Irish influence is one influence, but only one. Again, many of the Irish were of an Anglo-

Irish stock that accepted the British Empire, but had fallen foul of Cromwell. It probably is of significance, however, that in facilitating an economic model mediated in the English language, the Irish on Montserrat helped crush the links between the black slaves and Africa.

This raises an interesting question, one that has not been answered by Akenson and other scholars: if the Irish hegemony was complete, why are there so few residuals of the Irish language in the language of Montserrat? The answer may lie partially in the nature of the families involved in such a hegemony. The plantation class – the Tribes of Galway – would have had experience of suppressing Irish and enforcing the English language at home, both as a principle of affiliation with the coloniser and as a tactic for land and property retention.

The indentured servants and the transportees would have had a different experience in relation to the language. Unfortunately, we have no record of their experience. Akenson, in his recent book, acknowledges the Messengers' work of the sixties and seventies, but on the basis of his own analysis, and the research of others, disputes all the Messengers' indicators of Irishness. The Messengers' twelve residual effects were:

> Ubiquitous place-names
> Frequent Irish-derived family names
> Language inheritance
> Oral art, as in story-telling
> Musical styles
> Dance styles
> Pieces of ancient mythology
> Codes of etiquette and hospitality
> Illicit distilling and drinking

Specific foods
Motor patterns
System of values

Akenson finds none of these to have been proven as specifically Irish, except for possibly a mythological reference to the song/story 'The Mermaid of Chance Pool', and the bodhrán possibly being a source of the flat drum.

At one level, that of empirical verification, I agree with him, but all this is to confuse the manifestation of survival with the deeper functions of memory. It is a flaw of empiricist technique within a positivist method. The real issue is as to what function Irishness fulfils as an ethic, and politics of memory – and what it might release in Montserrat and Ireland. A point to which I will return.

Two recent works consider the Irish connection with Montserrat. *If the Irish Ran the World*, by Donald Harman Akenson, published in 1997, I have referred to already. The other one, and by far the greater achievement, is Howard Fergus's *Montserrat: History of a Caribbean Colony*, published in 1994. This latter, ranging from the earliest sources to the present day, is an engaged and engaging work of applied historical scholarship.

It has the merit, too, of not only including the historical work of Aubrey Gwynn, T. Savage English, John C. Messenger and Cullen, but also the more contemporary work of Lydia Pulsipher and R. Berleant-Schiller on the archaeology and the traces of the first occupants.

Fergus's work opens with a basic question: what is Montserrat, and who are the Montserratians? Born of the violence of nature, the island emerged as a volcanic outburst from the Caribbean. Its history is marked by the violence of tornadoes, hurricanes and volcanic eruptions that punctuate a game played against nature.

Hurricane Hugo in 1989 seemed at times to have played the final hand. It was resisted, and less than a decade later came the volcano. If nature had been resisted before, now onlookers saw in its eruption a new devastating, even a final, chapter for Montserrat.

But I know that this is not so, for Montserratians are the survivors of a struggle not only against the violence of nature, but also against all the man-made violences of colonialism, including its most vicious expression: slavery.

Some fundamental questions too may have been deferred, but they have not been abandoned, merely delayed, by the most recent tragic events, such as what cultural streams will inform Montserratian identity. Is a cultural independence possible? What shape will Montserratians put on the story of themselves? Part of that story will refer to an Irish connection. But that connection is itself capable, as I have said, to different tellings.

I went to Montserrat in 1985 to present a film that aimed to explore the Irish island of the Caribbean. It was a task that seemed simple from afar – and, from the perspective of journalistic writings of that time, an exotic project, one that titillated curiosity about the celebration of St Patrick's Day on an island in the Caribbean, an island that called itself the 'Irish Island'.

I could find gravestones and place-names with an Irish resonance. The shamrock stood as an equal symbol on Government House with the Union Jack. If the graves contained the bones of Ryans and Reillys, Dalys, Sweeneys, Tuites and O'Garas, they are the bones so often of descendants of black slaves who were given the names of their Irish Plantation owners: 'drivers', indentured servants, smallholders.

I recall asking myself in front of one of those gravestones: what of the lives of those 10,000 black slaves who occupied the island in 1787? Can their story be forgotten in some project of whimsical discovery? And what must their forefathers have felt two decades earlier when, in 1768, they walked to Government House on St Patrick's Day to revolt.

Expecting their Anglo-Irish masters to be lost in Celtic revelry, their plot was betrayed, as folk-history has it, by a domestic servant. They were cruelly executed. They died without a white hand raised in solidarity with them. Was it not the case that petty privilege was sufficient to woo the victims of colonisation from any common cause with the most exploited? But then race has so often easily defeated any conception of a common class.

Today, my memory is of such questions. But it is above all of an extraordinary friendliness whose equivalent I have never experienced more strongly elsewhere. My next most vivid memory is of the numerous decapitated sugar mills – symbols of the greed and madness that Europe's addiction to sugar unleashed on the lives of those torn from Africa, sold into slavery and treated like chattels.

Whence came the tradition, I asked myself, of conferring formal occasions with the wearing of a hat? And I recall the precociousness of the houses. It was as if everything was always being constructed: fresh gestures, eternal hope, as it always has been; as it must be again, after Hurricane Hugo; after the volcano's eruption; in the shadow of the volcano, life is being made anew.

That the Irish who came to the Caribbean were not all of similar capacity, in terms of wealth or opportunity, as those who would become plantation owners – the Blakes, the Lynches or the Kirwans, who would later be at the centre of a 'Plantocracy' built on the sugar trade and its terrible implement of inhuman abuse, slavery – is a fact that Howard Fergus notes.

Fergus tells us that 'There was a sharp distinction between this elite and lesser whites, although a few of the latter owned one or two slaves'. He further states:

> In 1678 only 26 percent of Montserratian householders were slave-owners, in contrast to 82 percent in Barbados in 1680. These second-class whites worked the subsistence economy, growing such cash crops as indigo, ginger, cotton, cocoa, coffee and cassava, which was staple eating. They constituted a free labour force working as carpenters and masons and at a variety of other trades associated with the sugar industry, the maintenance of posts and the catering and service sector.

Fergus's reference to the law of 1682, which was aimed at 'restricting Christians from federating with the Negros, and having convivial associations' is of particular importance in terms of what it reveals of a clear racist division. The law, of course, also points to a pattern of behaviour to which it sought to respond, and which must have existed.

His study of the structure of the sugar society and the related slavery are, for me, the most moving sections in Howard Fergus's work. The efforts he notes of the Plantocracy, the English and Anglo-Irish elite, to divide the second-class whites from slaves are of immense importance.

I am reminded of James C. Scott's *Domination and the Arts of Resistance: Hidden Transcripts*, published in 1990, which details the rich world that lay behind the deference that was forced from servants: the mask they were forced to wear and what feelings lay behind it. What of the cultural resistance, the stories and stratagems of those indentured servants, black slaves? Have we lost it? If, as it appears we have, it is a great loss. More importantly, it is a crucial part of what must be, perhaps imaginatively, recovered.

Returning to the early Irish settlers, the Irish malcontents were noted for their amenability to invading forces; a religious basis, perhaps more than the memory of dispossession, or any nationalist feeling, seems to have been the basis for this. That Louis XIV was briefly the monarch who ruled on Montserrat was in part owing to their complicity in invasions: in 1666/7, in 1710, and in 1782, for example. Future scholars will have to unravel the full story. Certainly it is too simple to relate the reasons for such attitudes as led to their availability for revolt against English rule being simply or exclusively religious ones.

The Irish then who came and lived on Montserrat came from an experience of dispossession, but there is no evidence that they saw any parallel between their position and that of the Arawaks or the Caribs who occupied the Caribbean so long before them. Their primary affiliation, in terms of valuing petty white privilege, which rejected class solidarity, and which has been recorded in 1768, should not surprise us. Noel Ignatiev's *How the Irish Became White*, published in 1995, makes chilling reading about the Irish North American opposition to Daniel O'Connell's denunciation of slavery. In so many different settings, race has defeated the forward movement of the solidarity of class.

However, if history is a teacher of anything, it is that there was no simple, single form of Irishness. I have to reject Akenson's view of the rational, calculating Irish, free to strike a bargain, of whom he wrote:

> The overwhelming majority of Irish indentured servants
> who went to Montserrat did so by personal choice, with

information in hand, and in fact made reasonable decisions as between two alternatives: remain at home or emigrate.

I believe he is tendentious in his over-simplification. Where is the evidence for such a generalisation? I am, however, interested in his reading of Pulsipher's work: that the Anglo-Celtic settlers destroyed the ecosystem of the island foot by foot as they introduced European agricultural techniques and practices for the exploitation of nicotine, indigo and sugar, and for precision growing.

There is on this island more than a regularly recovered, physical beauty. There is more than the task of physical reconstruction. Montserratians are the human survivors of a complex history, and within this tapestry of black and white, of blood and sweat, there is an emerald strand.

Montserrat does have an Irish dimension, an Irish connection. It is one that has been almost lost from the history books. It may be one strand in a complex history. It is not, to my mind, the most important, even if it reveals a bizarre twist in the story of colonisation – a story in some ways of the colonised becoming the coloniser.

Behind the physical comparisons, the place-names, the symbols, the folk takes and the emphasis on Irishness lies a complex storey. While it includes the Irish connection, this island was touched by every feature of colonisation: European conflicts, piracy, merchant ambition, competing evangelisation, and above all, slavery. It experienced all the traumas, the hopes and failures of post-emancipation attempts at reconstruction. Some prospects would be dashed by the fluctuating prices of commodities responding to European consumers' tastes, and perhaps the narrow nationalist policies of mercantilism. Others would be destroyed by tornados or earthquakes.

That is the setting for the Irish connection with Montserrat. An Irish connection that has been chosen today by Montserrat's administrators – more than 350 years after the first Irish arrived at Montserrat – as a major part of its identity, as a means of relating itself to its neighbouring islands and the wider world, whose visitors it seeks to attract. That Irishness is reflected in the symbols used for the stamping of passports for arrivals – a shamrock – or again, in other usages, a blonde-haired woman playing an Irish harp. Irishness exists in a sea of black Caribbean consciousness. The music today celebrates Africanness. But then both Irishness and black identity are assaulted by the daily popular media from the commercialised mass culture of the United States.

The Irishness of Montserrat is a story caught in a net of myths; myths which are perhaps fading today in conditions of rapid change. It is a story of such complexity that it is not widely understood. It may indeed never come to be fully known. The details of that story lie in archives in Ireland, Britain, France, Italy and the United States, in a number of religious houses, in private diaries and papers. Many records have been lost, and we rely at times on the folk history of earlier days.

We will never know if any survivors of the Touregue settlement on the Amazon, besieged and overrun by the Portuguese under Pedro Texeira, ever made it to Montserrat. We can accept that the first Irish were the settlers from St Kitts, and the later group of Irish malcontents from Virginia arrived between 1631 and 1635.

It was from the ranks of the Galway Tribes that the Irish adventurers who were to leave their names on plantations and estates came. The Blakes were typical. Their name still lives on in the island. It was the practice of Catholic landed families from County Galway to send a younger son to the West Indies to make his fortune.

The Galway Tribes, as they came to be rather benignly called in Irish history, had a unique connection with the West Indies. They were to use their fortunes from the West Indies to establish themselves in London. They were to be part of the commercial accumulation that made the British Industrial Revolution possible.

Cullen tells us that 'London houses arising from the colonial trade include those of the Blakes, Lynches, Kirwans, Hussey, Burke, Tuite, French, Skerrett, Digges La Touche, Nesbitt, Delap, Browne and Mead'. Undoubtedly, the Galway merchants predominated. But they were joined by Tipperary, Cork and Donegal families. But as Cullen tells us: 'all the Galway families first settled in the West Indies'.

The Galway merchant and landed gentry sent their younger sons here in search of fortune. While it is possible to see their money and their sons' arrival as a flight from persecution, it is more plausible to see it as an adventurer's pursuit of fortune. The case of Nicholas Tuite is illustrative:

> Nicholas Tuite was born in Montserrat in 1705, of Irish extraction, as were the majority of the colonists. In 1729 he owned 100 acres of land and forty-one slaves in that island. He also engaged in a variety of trades, one of which was a sloop trade in slaves and Irish provision to St Croix. After a hurricane ruined his property in Montserrat, he transferred his activities to St Croix. In 1776 he owned seven plantations there in his own right, and was part owner of seven others.
>
> He later became a West India Merchant of Lime Street, London. After his death in 1772, a London newspaper said that Tuite has encouraged seven hundred English families to purchase estates in St Croix. On a visit to Copenhagen in 1760, he was acknowledged as

the founder of the colony, the sole source of its greatness and the finest character of the realm. He was made Chamberlain to the King of Denmark. Nicholas Tuite left an estate of £20,000 per annum to his only son, Nicholas Tuite Selby, who became a London banker.

The graveyards of Montserrat carry the remains of some of the planters. Joining them are the graves of the indentured servants – really white slaves – who had chosen or been forced to sell themselves for a period of from five to seven years in expectation of a plot of land for 40 shillings.

Here too, perhaps, by way of the other Caribbean islands, came the products of the 'Houses of Correction'. Reports in England fulminated against Irish beggars, including those who paid 3 shillings to be brought illegally to England. Aubrey Gwynn has written of the political call for the implementation of the English Vagrancy Act of 1597 and to instructions given to the Justices of the Peace as to how to deal with 'Rogues, vagabonds and sturdy beggars'. They were to be 'stripped naked from the middle upwards, and openly whipped until his or her body be bloody, and then passed to his or her birthplace or last residence; and in case they know neither, they are to be sent to the Houses of Correction for a year, unless someone gives them employment sooner'.

It was, Gwynn tells us, 'from these Houses of Correction, usually erected, like the Earl of Cork's foundations, on the site of some dissolved friary, that English colonial traders with the West Indies drew many of their recruits for the labouring classes of the New World'.

Then too, Cromwell's subjugation of Irish towns in 1649/50 sent political prisoners to the West Indies. Dr Fergus feels that 'many reached Montserrat by way of Barbados, Virginia and St Christopher'.

It was in 1653 that the orders of transportation became frequent. There are orders for agents to carry 'vagrants, idle, incorrigible persons, sturdy beggars and the children of orphanages' to the New World for a life on the plantations.

On 20 January 1654, the governors of Carlow, Kilkenny, Clonmel, Wexford, Ross and Waterford are authorised to arrest all 'vagrants and rogues, men and women . . . and all such children as are in hospitals and workhouses, and all prisoners, men and women to be transported to the West Indies'.

From Galway, Colonel Stubbers was authorised on 26 June to 'transport out of Connaught for the West Indies three score Irish women that are vagrants, idlers and wanderers, that do not take themselves to some lawful way or means for their livelihood and subsistence'.

By now the demand for labour from the West Indies was virtually insatiable. A significant transition too had taken place, for, unlike the indentured servants, with the expectation if not the reality of fifteen shillings and a suit of clothes, the deportees of this period were offered nothing. For many, it was worse than death.

There was no discrimination in favour of age. A woman of over eighty is recorded as being sent out with her husband as an exemplary punishment. Children were sent. One woman begged to be 'sent into slavery' with her husband. She was refused.

Onto the shores of Montserrat, then, came those who were perceived as a threat, those who sought freedom from persecution. From a longer distance came those younger sons of the Irish merchants who hoped for a fortune, those who, like John Blake, had resolved 'to remove hence for Montserrat, and there to settle myself for some years, to the end I may in time gain something for to bring me at last home'.

There arrived there too from an equally long distance, but under cruel conditions, the conscripts, the political prisoners, the white indentured servants.

Those who came under the worst conditions, by direct or indirect routes, would find on their arrival that the plantations on which they would work were owned by their fellow townsmen, now firmly ensconced among the plantocracy. While Irish money and the younger sons of the Galway gentry had some choice in their destiny, Irish peasants, the Irish poor, the orphans, the political prisoners, had none.

Tobacco and sugar dominate the earlier period of the Irish connection. Addictive and unlimited in demand in Europe, it promised a fortune. Tobacco governed the lives of those who lived on the plantation, and these were white. The black slaves were yet to come. With the rise and fall in its price, the fortunes of the white planters rose and fell. But tobacco meant something else to those whites who slaved on the plantation. They had extracted from them as much labour as could be gained for the period of their indenture. Some died; others were worn out to a point close to death.

Writers differ as to whether this labour commodity in temporary ownership was treated even worse than the black slaves who were to follow, and who were owned, with their children, for life. The white slaves in the tobacco fields could hope for freedom, for a plot of land or even a small sum of money. The decline of tobacco and the arrival of the sugar economy of the Caribbean to Montserrat in 1650, with its land-intensive method of cultivation, was to remove even the prospect of a plot of land with freedom.

By 1664, the black slaves were being brought in in their thousands to work the sugar estates. By 1724, all land was in the hands of the large estate owners. Now many of them were absentee landlords. By 1729, many of the larger estates were consolidated in Irish ownership. Sugar was to transform the island.

Trant's estate was one of many plantations that would struggle with a difficult terrain and appalling difficulties to plant the canes and harvest their juice. Among the planters we discover a virtual roll-call of what a benign history has come to call the Merchant Tribes of Galway: Blakes, Brodericks, Lynches and Trants; they are joined by the Farrells, Ferguses, Furlongs, Lees, Mulcaires, O'Garas, Parsons, Reids, Rileys, Roches, Sweeneys, Tuites and Whites.

The most crucial piece of equipment of a sugar plantation was the mill. It was moved at different times in Latin America and the Caribbean by wind, water or cattle – or by slaves. The demand for sugar at its peak was to drive the plantation owners to a frenzy in their demands for productivity from their slaves. While the production in the West Indies in the first half of the eighteenth century would come to be regarded as the foundation of their greatness, as the addictions of tea and coffee were sweetened by sugar in Europe, those tastes, and that sweetness, were made possible from the blood of slaves.

While scholars can point to differences in styles of management between French and English plantation owners, they agree that these differences stemmed less from any humane impulses than from a desire for productivity. Indeed, a literature on plantation management and a school for planters' sons, which would include slave management, were to come into existence in the West Indies.

Children were quickly introduced to work. Orlando Patterson, writing of Jamaica, tells us:

> On some of the more benignly governed estates . . .
> they began working at the age of six, when they joined
> what was called the 'small gang', which, in addition to
> gathering grass from the stable, also carried green slips
> and vines to the hogs, under the supervision of an old

woman. On most estates, however, slaves began their working life between the age of four and five years. The 'Professional Planter', who was describing what he admitted to be the ideal condition, said they began working at the age of five, at which time the fruits of their labour was sufficient to defray the expense of their support.

Slaves in Jamaica worked an average of sixteen and a half hours per day throughout the year, and during the five months of crop, eighteen hours per day. In Montserrat it was hardly different. But Howard Fergus tells us that the transition from tobacco to sugar was slow:

> Montserrat's transition from tobacco, the first main crop, to sugar, was long, and both products continued to be the medium of barter and exchange until around 1685. Montserrat, the Roman Catholic asylum, did not attract many indentured servants. The supply of slaves in the middle of the seventeenth century was still small. Irish peasant growers held on to tobacco as long as they could. In 1680 the Council of Montserrat stated 'the scarcity of Negroes and white servants compelled the inhabitants to plant a little tobacco and indigo, both of inferior quality'.

With sugar came a transformation in land ownership. Small plots of 20 to 25 acres gave way to large estates of 500 to 700 acres and more. With sugar came slavery on a grand scale.

Tied to the land, owned by the landlord, their children born into slavery, punished at the whim of proprietary discretion, the thousands of blacks, kidnapped, bought and stolen from Africa, bartered by other planters, or perhaps the inherited commodities of wills, the means of settlement of gambling debts: blacks were regarded as chattels, listed in the inventory of estates with cattle and commodities.

In 1766, Broderick's plantation was sold by Michael White. He realised £12,000 for 200 acres of cane land at £60; £700 for a stone windmill; £28 for each of twenty-three mills; £240 for eleven head of cattle; and £11,080 for '224 Negroes at £45 sterling'. Dr Fergus also gives us details of the eleven slaves sold for £800 on the sale of Dominick Trant's estate on his death in 1762. Michael, a good cook, realised £120. The men ranged from £120 to £40. The women realised less. Bridget was sold for £55, and Clarissa for £60.

In 1726, an even more poignant account of a valuation of Delvin's plantation puts Negroes and cattle together. It also differentiates as to the relative strength of the slaves:

16 Negroes men (£40-£15 including Westmead, very sickly, £30) £475
17 Negro women (£40-£10 including Betty, sickly)   £477
13 children (£13-£3 for Susannah, an infant)   £91
Cattle 5 head of draft cattle   £45
Horses (including mare and two horses that can hardly walk) £48

Howard Fergus tells us that 'in 1680 the Council of the Island was lamenting the lack of slaves. In 1672 there were 523. In 1678 there were 922, of whom 292 were children. By 1707 there were 3,570; 1,604 were imported between 1698 and 1707. By 1774 there were 10,000. Montserratian planters tried to pay for slaves with sugar – to barter for them – and slavers were not keen to do business on such terms. Slave stealing too among planters was common and had to be prohibited by ordinance'.

Montserrat is fortunate in having in Dr Howard Fergus, a

resident historian of great calibre, somebody with the scholarly rigour and commitment required to recover the history of the island in its darkest hours, as well as its general history. His account tells of the punishments meted out to slaves by planters:

> For stealing stock, cattle, equipment to the value of twelve pence current money, a slave shall suffer a severe whipping and have both ears cut off for the first time, but for the second offence shall in like nature suffer death in the form aforesaid.

Alan Burns is quoted by Dr Fergus as giving the example of a slave convicted of the theft of nine pigs being sentenced to be cut to pieces; another, for having fresh meat in his home for which he cannot render account, is to have his right ear cut off and is to be burned on his breast with an iron. Striking a white man brought death.

> In 1754 a Negro boy, Tom Boy, entered a house and, taking bread, the fact having been partly proved, was ordered to be whipped and both his ears cut off. In 1785 two slaves, Tom Kirwan and Hannah Woods, the property of Nicholas Hill, were convicted of stealing sundry pieces of wearing apparel worth ten shillings. Tom was sentenced to transportation, while Hannah received thirty-nine lashes in the pillory.

Among the slaves, division was sown on the basis of tasks, with the black slaves doing the most arduous tasks on the land. They were classed like cattle. Above them were those who avoided manual work. Other differences in petty priorities, too, were based on colour. Progression towards purchasing freedom meant moving away from the soil and the hardest labour. It meant too, for some, rejection of being black, being African. Black was the symbol of the cruellest labour, the harsh land and death.

A simple view would see both victims of oppression – white indentured slaves, forced or torn from their homelands, and black slaves, now in their thousands and outnumbering whites, snatched and sold from their homelands – as able to make common cause.

Indeed, planter worries were on the increase as their numbers as a class dwindled. Plantation owners were to devise strategies of dividing the black slaves, buying them from different traders, from different language groups. They thus exploited divisions between native-born and bought-in slaves. They established categories of status between some indentured whites and blacks through creating posts as overseers, foremen or drivers as they became trained.

This allowed white slaves access to the marketplace with their surplus. They were to perceive any literacy among blacks as a tool of subversion – something to be resisted. They were also to be excluded from evangelisation into Christianity. This too could encourage subversion. In particular, it lost the productivity of blacks for at least part of Sunday.

Slaves were denied any music or entertainment of a collective kind. Reflecting their insecurity too in a growing sea of black slaves, planters forbade the beating of drums, casks or gourds, and the blowing of shells or loud instruments. All entertainment for slaves was forbidden.

One cannot, as I have said, but speculate as to whether there was any white shame at the lack of solidarity between black and white oppressed when, on St Patrick's Day in 1768, the slaves revolted. Expecting their masters to be revelling, they had planned that the domestic servants would relieve the gentlemen of their swords. The others would storm the house.

The plot was betrayed, it is believed, by a female domestic

servant. The leaders were executed. Who were among the slaves? Who were with the executing planters? The likelihood is that the Irish planters, as part of the plantocracy into which they were wedded and connected in so many ways, were on the side of the executioners. It is equally plausible that, divided by status, occupation and colour, the brave black slave leaders were without the support of the white Irish oppressed.

Divided by status, motivated by private ambitions, conscious of colour, bought off by the petty privileges of the plantation society, they did not see, or chose not to see, a common cause with the most oppressed of the oppressed. It would be nice to think that it had been different.

Always on Montserrat there has been an unending game with nature. In 1773, there was a disastrous hurricane. In 1843 an earthquake; another hurricane in 1899; hurricanes in 1924 and 1928; an earthquake in 1974; and Hurricane Hugo in 1989; in recent years the volcanic eruptions have been devastating.

While volcanic eruptions are rare, hurricanes constitute a regular threat, punctuating efforts at building an island economy. Thus it was with limes. Lime-growing started in 1852 and covered 600 acres by 1878. A cure for scurvy in the estimation of admirals, for their sailors, it gave the world the appellation of 'limey' for an Englishman. In more polite society, temperance movements recommended it as an alternative to the 'demon' alcohol. In refined circles, magazines announced that 'In the summer, my lady drinks Montserrat lime juice'.

In 1885, 1,000 acres was under cultivation, and 180,000 gallons of juice were exported. Then came the hurricane of 1899. By 1900, the estates were empty, and Montserrat's days of lime were over.

After limes came cotton, now a struggling industry. And selective tourism too. The economic future of Montserrat is likely to require a continuation of both emigrants' remittances and a British grant-in-aid. But others should also assist, for there is a Montserratian reality that will emerge and enhance the Caribbean.

When I visited in the mid-eighties, and when a friend, Peter Butler, took his first photographs a few years later, it was before Hurricane Hugo and before the volcanic eruption. If eleven people were killed by Hugo, it was less than previous disasters. The fact that Montserratians are practical and were prepared is responsible for the relatively small number of lives lost. The images of devastation have to be weighed against the resilience of a people who are always in the act of reconstruction. And if the decapitated sugar mills dotted the Montserratian landscape when I visited in the eighties, there was an energy too that was visible everywhere.

That energy was reflected in the building of houses, but more so in the presentation of self. When the bells of the myriad of churches called out on Sunday, they drew forth a mixture of hats that was as colourful as the flora of Montserrat. If that flora has been captured in the wonderful stamps of Montserrat, the spirit of Montserratians is more elemental.

It has always been in survival colours that Montserratians have defeated history. Their place – Montserrat – is secure because it has a moral lodgement in the imagination of historians everywhere. There is on Montserrat a human testament that is so obvious. It goes beyond any principle of survival. It shows itself in the confident love of children. Montserratians in the past have borne the burden of emigration and a precarious economic existence; the Montserrat of the future will accord them, I hope, a proper place.

Emigration, as in Ireland, has been the answer to the imbalance between population and life expectations. As in the case of the Irish, more Montserratians live abroad than at home. The descendants of the colonised are to be re-colonised as a mobile labour force in a world of ever more mobile investment. There is no place for the sentimental in reflections on Montserrat's future. All choices will be hard. But Montserratians will choose what is best for Montserratians. That is as it should be.

Should Monserratians choose to eschew the Irish threads in their history – those first Irish adventurers, or those deported to their shores in the seventeenth century – it will be understandable. I feel that they will not. The construction of the past that informed this sense of the present while I visited was enormous.

Their future will, I hope, bring excitement by not only telling their own story in their own way and providing a home on their beautiful island for future generations of Montserratians, but also by accepting in a sophisticated way that there are no pure forms of the relationship between coloniser and the colonised, as Albert Memmi has shown us. Indeed, we must learn too from the fact that it is part of our history that some Irish, victims themselves of colonisation, while colonised in exile, visited on others the worst excesses of that of which they themselves had suffered, or became lost in adventurous greed.

The lesson for us all is to have the courage to live with uncertainties but never to allow an economic model of the market to defeat our most basic human solidarities, never again to let racial difference rationalise exploitation and subjugation in the service of greed.

St Patrick's Day is celebrated in Montserrat today with the warmest feelings of friendliness, an invocation of Irishness, and the stressing of common bonds. Yet behind this achievement in the transcendence of memory lies a dark narrative of petty race and privilege defeating class solidarity. Those who remain on Montserrat today are renowned for their friendship. It is a friendship that must in the recent past have contained a great act of forgiveness. They must not be required to affect an amnesia, however. An amnesty on what cannot be agreed, or what is too awful to concede, is sufficient, and more moral.

Today's inhabitants are the descendants of those torn from Africa, sold into slavery, press-ganged from Bristol, or forced into indentured service – descendants of an extraordinary struggle for survival. The search for an identity, too, while it might contain a sense of Africa, Britain and Ireland, must direct itself also towards an uncertain further. For even in the midst of natural disasters, the question of contemporary identify is raised. That independence will involve a choice of identity with which to relate not only to the Caribbean but to the world, and to the Montserratian diaspora.

It may be too much to hope on the first St Patrick's Day of a new millennium, but it might still be our prayer in the shadow of a great survival by the colonised cousins in Montserrat.

On St Patrick's Day, I am reminded that Irishness needs an ecumenical definition. It is a creation of exile as much as, if not more than, the received tradition of a sedentary pool of undisturbed natives. What is richest comes perhaps from the interstices. Cultural expressions were revised, reinvented and revived in Ireland, and of course, more importantly, in the coming and going, what is cultural in Irishness has been enriched.

We share the experience of exile with Montserratians. They, like us, are called to reinvent themselves, to recreate their imaginative space. Again, making a new identity for a new world of integrated markets is both a challenge and an opportunity. It is a challenge to fashion a cultural diversity that would withstand the commodification of every aspect of our lives.

The globalisation of the media world is the sugar industry of our times. In pursuing issues of our complex identities, and those points where they intersect, we have to create the principles of an honest amnesty rather than sheltering under an evasive amnesia.

So I recall today the bravery of the leaders of 1768 – the forced labourers, the involuntary exiles of both our countries – and I can offer an understanding, but nothing more than an amnesty, to the Irish malcontents who in 1779 were a core of Montserrat's plantation elite. Before our own famine of 1847, they were gone from Montserrat, proof that there is nothing more mobile than speculative capital.

This obdurate fact of Montserrat life is well caught by one of Montserrat's poetic voices: Archie Markham, in his poem 'Homecoming':

> The man peered at me across
> his life and apologised
> in a voice I have sometimes used
> in victory.
> 'It's abandoned,'
> he said. 'No one comes here now.'
> I used to work your father's
> land, in the old days. The disappearing
> patch of garden, the orphaned fruit –
> trees, the 'ruin' from a past
> decade tugged my memory back
> to childhood. The revelation rinsed
> my mind and his face
> like spray from a hose: he stood unmasked,
> the bright lad in the class giving
> the right answer, his face
> comic, furrowed like the land

then out of fashion. How with neglect,
erode, Past Tense like the generation
of our fathers – exposed roots
and veins in a bald skull – the face
like the land of my landless father
presents me with the task
of reparation. Who is this old man,
my age.

15.

'Monkeys in the Superstructure': Peadar O'Donnell

In introducing Peadar O'Donnell, I know that I will probably say some things that he would not say himself, because he has taken recently to the strategy of dismissing his own activities and emphasising the importance of the issues with which he has been identified: the importance of courage, the importance of consistency, the importance of not inventing optimism but of discovering it and seeing the places within human affairs where there is an optimistic interpretation of the forward move of history.

Peadar O'Donnell was born on 22 February 1893 in Meenmore, near Dungloe, County Donegal. In his long career he has been a teacher, a migrant worker, a writer. He has served on commissions; he has travelled abroad and lectured to international movements; he has served on the secretariat of organisations. In all this he has been a socialist republican. In the works that have been published about his life he has stressed – I think – his own role as that of being, above all else, an agitator in the very best sense; that is, exposing the comfort and the cosiness which people have used as a shell to mask exploitation from the gaze to which it should be subjected.

People talking about Peadar O'Donnell have usually adopted the strategy of selecting some aspect of his life for particular mention. Some concentrate on his work as a writer. There is a substantial body of material from which they could draw, be it in terms of the political and social pamphlets he wrote, or of the moving descriptions of life that he published. Early in his life, for example, he wrote of immigrants who had been burned to death. The victims were from his native Donegal, and had been forced to work in Scotland in appalling conditions.

There are his novels also, moving on from *Storm*, published in 1925, through *Adrigoole*, *On the Edge of the Stream*, *The Big Windows* and *The Knife*, to his last, powerful novel, *Proud Island*.

But there are others, in turn, who would stress his long political career, which in Ireland alone has identified itself with translating the project of nationalism into something that should have a social and radical content. To move beyond territorial independence into a genuine independence that would transform social and political relationships.

Others would move beyond his national political and social contribution, and stress his long relationship with the opposition to fascism. Peadar O'Donnell was in Berlin in the late 1920s and could watch the rise of Hitler. He was among those who worked for the tiny band of people – less than two hundred – who went to defeat fascism in Spain. Intervening in all this were periods spent in prison. There were times on hunger-strike.

I prefer not to choose between these divisions, as he himself rejected always the division of life and art. His life has been dedicated to establishing an integration in all these things, to giving the lie, if you like, to the terrible division which has made so much of our own work as teachers useless. So much of our witness as intellectuals is meaningless because we have been instructed to divide what we do at the level of mind from the level of action. He has been somebody who combined the work of a writer with a radical commitment to the social context from which he was drawing his literary material. The audience to which his work was directed was not isolated and given precedence. He established a unique integration in that way. He has said to one of his biographers: 'I would like to be remembered less as a writer than as an agitator.' In fact, he is described by Bowyer Bell as probably the greatest Irish agitator of this century.

It is in that sense that he has made his signal contribution. Not only in the integration of mind and heart and action; he has also drawn attention to the divisions in Ireland, between our consciousness, our action and our organisational aims. The divisions that have stopped us achieving the project of true liberation, the establishment of a new, liberal, pluralist, non-sectarian and egalitarian society. He has argued for the combination in our perspectives of the realities of rural life and of urban life. He has written of the necessity for Labour having courage and not missing its historic tasks; of republicanism accepting the necessity for its socialist dimension if it was to achieve its full purpose. He has suggested how important it is not only to seek to achieve national projects but also to look at the great international issues of the day. It is that that brought him – as I said – to oppose fascism from its inception.

And to Spain. And much later on, when neo-fascism was surfacing again, to lend his voice to movements that were important in modern Irish history, such as the opposition to the Vietnam war, to the cruel terror that was perpetrated on the people of Vietnam.

This isn't, then, so much a polite occasion for me, as a moving occasion, because this meeting is taking place in a university on the occasion of our recalling and celebrating our objection to the granting of an honorary doctorate in law to somebody [US president Ronald Reagan] whom we believe to be possibly one of the most significant threats to peace in modern times. Someone who mocks the idea of law itself, be it in an international sense, through the threat to small, sovereign neighbouring countries. A sponsor of terrorism on the borders of the country's neighbour Nicaragua, Peadar O'Donnell himself was precluded from entering the United States for most of his life. He was also – something which we have to bear continually in mind – banned from entering the gates of a university. When I was a student, it was impossible for Peadar to accept an invitation to UCD, for example. One of his first appearances after his long ban was, in fact, in a hall in UCG when he spoke about the unfinished tasks of organising rural and urban Ireland in the direction of radical solutions to their problems.

There is another quality beyond this quality of integration that is one of the most important aspects of Peadar O'Donnell's life. He continually stresses in the interviews he has given that he wants to be remembered less for the things that he did as an individual than for the movements of people as social groups that he facilitated and in which he participated. He has assumed many roles, then: as a schoolteacher, as a trade union organiser, as a social reformer, a writer, novelist, historian and agitator; as someone who in the editorials of *An Phoblacht* between 1924 and 1930 made the case in print for radicalism to one of the widest audiences for such a message ever in this country, when the circulation was beyond 50,000. Subsequently it was as editor of *The Bell*, receiving articles and courageously rejecting the shutters that had come down on our mind, and expressing the importance of opening our minds to other enriching ideas, and to be responsive to the great moral issues of the day. Peadar made an inestimable contribution.

And his life was not one of unending success. The fact that we are celebrating him here is as much – I think – to join with him in tribute to the things in which he did not succeed completely, or to the people for whom he wanted success but who have had to wait.

He is the president of the Irish Academy of Letters at the moment [in 1984]; together with Seán O'Faoláin and Francis Stuart, he is one of the three surviving members of that academy, founded by Yeats and Shaw in 1932. In the world of letters, he has given a unique testament to the importance of not making literature itself something separate from life, something directed to a minority audience, or something for which you could – for example – achieve some kind of special excellence of competence that was contextually separate from the themes with which it deals. Even in the analysis of his novels, the evidence is there, and it is rich. In what is regarded as his greatest novel, *The Big Windows*, for example, all the main characters are women. He had a unique insight into the mind of women – which is available for anybody to see in that book, which appeared in print in the 1950s.

In the conversation between the mother and her daughter-in-law from the island, who cannot come to live with the shadows on the mountains, and for whom her husband puts in the big windows, the phrase occurs 'that a man must be good to his neighbours but he must have a good greed for the world in him'. Peadar was aware of the fact that in literature one should not really speak about the personal destruction of characters. It was his great achievement that he established probably a unique contribution to social realism and socialist realism in our time. Certainly he eschewed modish ruralism and sentimentality.

The events in the novels themselves are explained and made understandable in terms of the ingress of greed on the lives of the community, and what is possible from the power of the community. This vision in his novels is perfectly consistent with his early writing; for example, when he was describing the bothy-fire disaster of 1937:

The world says it was a rock, and the world says it was a fog. But it was not a rock, it was society. The world has spelled out one of its crimes in corpses. But if the agony of that moment of breathed prayer, that comes as close to us as our breathing, does not flash into a decision to end the impounding of the Gael and the trek to the Scottish tatie fields, then the suggested beacons around Aranmore are not a remedy, but a hush-hush to ease settled consciences.

When we ourselves wanted to jog consciences therefore, and draw attention to the travesty that it was to give a doctorate of laws in all our names to somebody who is a threat to peace, it was logical that we would turn to Peadar O'Donnell, one who had jogged the conscience of the Irish people, nationally and internationally, in so many different ways, so well, for so long, and with such patience.

There will be, for all of you who wanted to read his work, so many other values that you can draw out of it. There is the optimism that sometimes frustrated many of his friends, who felt that the projects were not succeeding. There is the message in his book on the land annuities campaign: 'There will be another day.' I believe that Peadar O'Donnell, in the integration he has established in a world whose divisions had made us often impotent, has made an inestimable contribution. He has been like a rock – I believe myself – retaining humour and always stressing that to make an abstract or theoretical analysis is totally insufficient. His message has been that you must know that the project of your life and your fellows is the undoing of exploitation, that you must anchor it in the movements that can bring that about; that you must educate and bring people with you; that you must agitate; and that you must do so with humility and patience, accepting reverses as only temporary reverses, and having confidence in the future, historical liberation that will bring and establish true peace, bring a true liberation and sovereignty of the human spirit. This is not a case for utopianism. It is an invitation to work with mind and heart, totally in the world.

It is for all that that Peadar O'Donnell worked so patiently. Whether it was as a member of the League of Writers for Peace and Against Fascism, or as a member of the European Farmers Confederation, so long ago in so many different East European countries, we express our gratitude and solidarity this evening. It is very appropriate, it is very proper, that we would honour this man above all for a commitment to one profound insight: that it is not in the satisfaction of the individual tendency that true progress comes about, but in a social transformation that respects and honours the dignity of one's fellow workers in the struggle. For all these reasons: '*Is Onoir more dom iarraidh ar Pheadar O'Donnell labhairt libh anocht.*'

Introduction to Monkeys in the Superstructure: Reminiscences of Peadar O'Donnell, *1984*

16.

Remembering Bobbie Burke

It is appropriate that tribute is being paid to Bobbie Burke, one of the great names of which Tuam can be proud. If, in the modern period, Tuam has served as background to some of the most important work of one of the most important writers for the theatre in modern times, Tom Murphy, it can probably claim the most committed idealist of the early decades of the twentieth century.

The cause of Labour was adopted by Bobbie Burke as his choice from a number of competing political ideologies that were available to him as a young man, nurtured in what was called Christian Socialism. He joined the party at the instigation of Jack Coughlan in 1932. Indeed, I recall that it was Jack Coughlan who first introduced me to the legacy in Labour history left by Bobbie Burke.

When the Labour Branch was being revived at the end of the 1960s and into the early 1970s, some members wanted the branch to be called the St Joseph's branch of the Labour Party. I believe myself that this probably had more to do with the local significance of St Joseph's Labour Hall, the building of which was a project which Bobbie Burke had helped initiate, rather than any excess of piety addressed towards St Joseph the worker.

The Labour Party was privileged to have been the choice of Bobbie Burke. The party itself was just twenty years old and had the marks of divisions left by the decisions not to contest the 1918 general election and the later decision to help form the new parliamentary system that had followed the Civil War.

Bobbie Burke had joined Labour just as Mr de Valera was agreeing to enter the Dáil. In his first election, the snap election of 1933, called by Mr de Valera so as to secure an overall, clear majority, Bobbie Burke got over three thousand votes.

This was not surprising in one sense. He had after all been an activist and ceaseless letter writer to the local papers on such issues as unemployment, bad housing, inadequate wages and neglect of social provision in general in rural Ireland. On the other hand, he faced resentment because of his background as a landlord, his Protestant faith, and something which has been much underestimated: the fact that his successful agricultural co-operative efforts could be branded as a form of 'Protestant Communism', and that his efforts, indeed his real achievements, in providing housing for workers and poorer people, had a sinister purpose – that in fact it was an attempt at proselytization.

The 1930s was a period of intense sectarian and repressive discourse and indeed legislation, of which the 1934 Dance Halls Act was a symbol, ending as it did crossroads dancing. The publication of the papal encyclical *Quadragesimo Anno* in 1931 had given an impulse to vocationalism and it is to the great credit of Bobbie Burke that he was willing to support and become involved in the socially beneficial work of such new organisations as Muintir Na Tíre and other organisations that had a clear Roman Catholic clerical hegemony.

Bobbie Burke served on the Administrative Council of the Labour Party in 1933, worked on its policy documents and gave one of the most important speeches to the 1934 conference on the topic of the necessity and merits of small farmers co-operating so as to be able to get the benefits of new machinery and efficient production.

He saw the possibility of producing for the sugar factory as a great opportunity. He was to stand again for the party in 1937 in what had become a four-seat constituency, with one of the seats spoken for through the occupancy of the Ceann Comhairle, thus making it effectively a three-seater. He increased his vote but was not successful.

He stood again in 1943 and, although securing over five thousand votes, was not successful. He had, however, been elected to Galway County Council in 1942 with a huge vote. He retained his seat in 1947 and in 1948. After an unsuccessful attempt in the general election he was, however, elected on the Agricultural Panel to the Seanad where he once again introduced his ideas on the importance of agricultural co-operation and innovation.

When one reviews his speeches in the Seanad, the themes that occur again and again are the importance of appropriate wages, the right to free time, annual holidays, insurance and the equitable distribution of wealth.

He was immensely popular in the Seanad, but for some this represented a danger. They liked the man, but were apprehensive about the ideas. On the occasion of his proposing a motion in March 1950, Senator S. O'Farrell had this to say:

> I do not suggest that Senator Burke comes in here with a sickle and hammer in his attaché case. I do not suggest that he has a red flag wrapped around him. I know that he is the most inoffensive person here. I know that he is the mildest mannered man – I will not finish that quotation. He has never said or done

anything offensive and because of that, he is very popular and because of that he is very dangerous. He can
very easily get people to agree with things that are not
worthy of support.

The debate in question was in my view one of the finest exposi-
tions of farming in Ireland ever given in a parliamentary debate.
Senator Burke gave details of the accounts from Toghermore, the
agricultural practices, the working arrangements and the social
conditions.

He outlined in little less than a brilliant way, the advantages of
farmers working co-operatively. He gave suggestions for the
improvement of agricultural practices. What is interesting is the
degree to which one speaker after another makes claims as to the
inherent individualism of the Irish farmer and the distrust of the
state.

It was probably obvious in 1948 that even though the
Toghermore experiment was a success as reported by Bobbie Burke,
speaking in the Seanad, those who listened to him were anxious to,
at most, allow such experiments to be just that, experiments. There
was of course the odd ignoramus who shouted about the 'Socialists
in the Seanad' and the 'Communists' as one interruption put it. In
the event, the motion was withdrawn in the absence of support.

After the transfer of the lands to the Land Commission and on
to the Co-operative members, the experiment was over, but Bobbie
Burke was to go on with his commitment to humanity and the
decades of contribution to Tuam and Ireland were to be followed by
further decades of contribution from his well of Christian
Socialism, to Nigeria, Kenya and finally Yemen.

For any of those who met him it was a privilege. For citizens
of Tuam, his life remains as a testament to what is possible, if

unattained. And for those of us in the Labour Party, we are honoured that he was one of one of us and we will always treasure both the man and his extraordinary contribution to life as it might and should be lived.

Address at the opening of Bobbie Burke Commemoration Events,
Tuam, 12 October 2007

17.

Remembering Noel Browne

'You would have to go back, I suppose, into the whole of my life to wonder why it was that I can't disengage myself . . . . I have been unable to get any kind of emotional peace, any kind of emotional satisfaction. If that is a messianic complex, then I suppose it is part of my personality . . . . I have been unable when what I feel is human suffering or degradation, humiliation or their avoidable unhappiness . . . to pass by on the other side. As a psychiatrist, I should know more about myself as a person . . . unfortunately I haven't been able to do it.' (Gerry Gregg, 1981)

This quotation reflects an engagement with the world that is as profoundly humanist as it is certain to bring the pain of having engaged with an unrealisable ethic in any conservative capitalist society. The statement is particularly exceptional in our own times of declining solidarity, fragmented experience, insatiable consumption, individualism and broken communities.

It is perhaps the most valuable aspect of John Horgan's book [*Noel Browne: Passionate Outsider*] that it patiently assembles the material on Noel Browne that has been scattered across tapes and theses and that it supplements such material with interviews and letters from surviving relatives, friends and acquaintances. It will for this reason alone be an indispensable starting point for further work on the period and its personalities.

I believe it to be of great importance, however, not to see this work as a corrective to either Noel Browne's *Against the Tide* or indeed Phylis Browne's description of her life with Noel. *Against the Tide*'s opening chapters are poetic. They are of a quality that reminds us of Jean-Paul Sartre's recounting of his childhood or of Proust's *Á La Recherche du Temps Perdu* . . .

In the preface to *Against the Tide*, Noel Browne clearly states that he is recovering a life back through the filter of time. That is why the book relied in the early passages on sense memory. The events experienced with the greatest sensory range are recalled in the greatest detail . . . particulars from childhood experience.

John Horgan's *Noel Browne: Passionate Outsider* is, on the other hand, a project in the craft and art of biography. It assembles contextual material and does not shirk from conclusions. I find myself agreeing with the views on memory and trauma, for example, drawn from an interview with Ivor Browne. (I entirely disagree, incidentally, with the works quoted on the influence position in family may have had in the case of the Browne family. I may be wrong, but I recall this research being drawn from much more cohesive family settings than those evoked in the Browne circumstances.)

It is the privilege of the biographer to present us with the fully rounded person who is the subject of his research. That task will inevitably reveal maybe as much about the biographer as the subject.

As a former parliamentarian, John Horgan has an advantage in being able to elicit the nuance behind the formal language of parliamentary party meetings and administrative council resolutions in the period before the sanitising rinse of press officers had been seen as essential. He has used his experiences well, and his skills as a distinguished journalist have been applied with good effect in terms of readability.

As to the subject of the book, I regard it as a privilege to have known Dr Noel Browne. I look at all the events recounted in this book through the lens of friendship, which requires an even greater ethic than justice.

My memory, in later years, is of a person of extraordinary grace, charm and consideration. For example, the comparison of Noel's letters to the *Irish Times*, his speeches, his denunciations, with the language of the cyclostyled document *Is It Needed?* would disqualify Noel Browne from consideration as the author of that document. In thirty years I never recall him using a word such as 'scum': his vocabulary was much better endowed.

The photographs in the book show his extraordinary handsome face. Robbie Harvey's photos in particular emphasise his long fingers, and he had a beautiful smile.

As to later years, I can confirm that I had no interest in standing for the presidency in 1990. Emmet Stagg and I proposed Dr Browne's name, and when defeated, enthusiastically supported the campaign of Mary Robinson. The description of me, in the biography of our former president, as being unenthusiastic, is unworthy of the informant, and untrue.

John Horgan's book has the benefit of the McQuaid papers being available. A younger generation will benefit from reading those extracts that show an authoritarian and devious attempt to subvert a public health policy.

In relation to another source, I believe Noel Browne is entitled to an apology. His version of the circumstances of the declaration of the Irish Republic has been the version vindicated by such subsequent papers as have become available. When the controversy occurred, he was practically called a liar.

After *Against the Tide*, Noel began a new set of writings. They were in short-story form. They revealed what I believe was an extraordinary talent for details, for compression of experience, and the invocation of atmosphere.

This writing was not emotion recollected in tranquillity. It was an imaginative achievement in the use of memory: no mere rational reconstruction, but work enriched by emotion.

It is those who do not avert their gaze, who internalise the pain and grief of the other, who can give us the fullest, most liberating, if upsetting, version of what it is we lose when we settle for a lesser version of ourselves and our world. That is the gift – a priceless one – of the dissenting mind, of which we have had too few.

Noel's moral and intellectual courage was exceptional, and I am glad in particular that a younger generation will have an opportunity through this biography of engaging with his life and times, of discovering courage, and changing the world.

Address at the launch of John Horgan's
Noel Browne: Passionate Outsider
at the National Museum of Ireland, 16 October 2000

18.

'A Celebration of the Divine in Nature and the Senses': Of My Friendship with John O'Donohue

Being a friend of the late John O'Donohue was a special experience: a blessing. His presence preceded any words that might later be exchanged. He had a capacity to create a reassurance and make a bridge of understanding that was instinctive, pre-verbal.

He visited me frequently during my stay in hospital in 2005. Before I opened my eyes, I knew he was there. At this time he was working on a lecture for John Dillon's seminar on neo-Platonism. He was preparing his paper, later published as a pamphlet under the title 'Towards a Poetics of Possibility'. We discussed utopian studies, hope, possibility, and Ernst Bloch, before, seeing my energy ebbing, he told me to keep my spirits up and left with a typical John O'Donohue invocation and blessing. For so many, he was a special friend.

I had suggested to him earlier that he should write a book on friendship. I felt that his previous work and his ongoing great project, a work on Meister Eckhart, had prepared the ground. He was, however, reluctant to embark on anything that might delay the big work on Eckhart. My suggestion was made after I had launched *Divine Beauty* for him.

In a foreword to a new publication of John's first poems, *Echoes of Memory*, Lelia Doolan quotes John's mother's remark in 2003. 'Ah poor John, Beauty has him killed!' After *Divine Beauty*, the major work was his focus.

The book on friendship was not to be. It remains my hope, and the hope of so many others, that his work on Meister Eckhart can be completed by some appropriate scholar. In the meantime, *Echoes of Memory* has just appeared.

This is an early John O'Donohue, but all the central themes of the later works are present.

Echoes of Memory was first published by Salmon Publishing in 1994 and has just now been published in a handsome hardback edition by his publishers Transworld. It appears after his untimely death in January 2008 and, of course, after such works as *Anam Cara*, *Eternal Echoes*, *Divine Beauty* and *Benedictus*.

Echoes of Memory has a thematic connection to all these works as well as to John's lesser-known *Towards a Poetics of Possibility*, written just three years before his passing. The vindication of memory runs through all the works as a recurring theme. In memory is lodged not only what was experienced but also what was imagined as possible. Possibility was not the stuff of fantasy but rather the human spirit in the midst of that which challenged and contradicted it.

The poems in the collection show further the value that John saw in the definition of what was truly human as being part of a divinity shared with nature. This profound and actual humanity he brought to friendship. Friendship consisted of a celebration, a shared divinity located in every living thing. Such a version of divinity allowed for a form of fragile intimacy. Nor was nature exhausted by the encounter. The human subject was stretched into such a context of time and space as allowed for the dignity of a life, but reminded of its transitory nature.

The poems in the recent publication, *Echoes of Memory*, reflect this. These are the poems of a young man working within ancient categories and contradictions, including engaging with the cultural rituals that seek to resolve such an unavoidable paradox as that of our possessing an infinite imagination but a finite physical life. These contradictions are engaged without any descent into sentiment.

Running right through the four sections, and the more than fifty poems, is a commitment to the truth of the senses. The senses are the source of the spiritual legacy that later philosophical work would see as that legacy of a life.

It is because the senses are recognised that exile and the desert experience can be understood. So, too, the journeying between the warmth of human hearths and bleak rock is recognised in such poems as 'Taken', written in memory of his father:

> Were you able
> To sense the loss
> Of colours, the yellows
> And cobalt blue that you loved,
> The honey scent of seasoned hay
> You carried through the winter
> To cattle on the mountain?

As I read these poems of my friend who passed on in untimely death, I thought of the poem of Wordsworth, 'Michael', and in particular of the line that ends 'and never lifted up a single stone'. The sheepfold would never be finished. The father had lost his companion son to the city. There is a similar sense of loss in John O'Donohue's evocation of rural tasks and intimacies.

In 'Voices at the Funeral', human strategies of transition between life and death make the basis of a reflection that presents the body for burial as a vessel of life, but not the totality of life:

Neighbours lay her out, wash her beads of life-sweat.
True to custom, don't throw this water out,
But distribute it to plants she grows.

In John O'Donohue's poems there is no descent to the pseudo-pastoral. The hard edge of intellect informing heart is retained. Memory is a recurrent theme, sometimes as sensory recall of sensations lost, of beauty that was ephemeral, but, perhaps most important of all, in terms of John O'Donohue's later work, as a sacred repository of all that had been the stuff of hope, the promise of possibility.

The last section in *Echoes of Memory* – 'Icons of Love' – is anticipated in the collection by such an early poem as 'Woman and Steel', but the later section is concentrated on a delicate, sustained, beautiful and erotic set of poems that deal with love and intimacy.

Reading the poems, I feel the loss of a friend who was overflowing with life at its most powerful and compassionate, but at the same time I am grateful for these fragments, which, taken together, make a powerful testament to a life so rich but ended too soon. These poems are the early promise of a life given generously, given to all who met John. Evidence of a unique openness to vulnerability, joy and our fragile earth, they will obdure, as will our memories of him.

Delivered on 26 October 2009, on the occasion of the republication of John O'Donohue's early poems, Echoes of Memory

Index